# HUNTSPUR
## AND
## ALONG THE TRACKS

*A History of Huntspur, Michigan
and Interviews with Early Residents of the Area*

# HUNTSPUR

## AND

### ALONG THE TRACKS

*A History of Huntspur, Michigan
and Interviews with Early Residents of the Area*

**BY**

**JANE KOPECKY**

Edited by Tyler Tichelaar

Technical Assistant Susanne Barr
Layout Stacey Willey
Globe Printing, Inc., Ishpeming, MI
www.globeprinting.net

ISBN 978-0-9905140-0-8
© June 2014 - Jane Kopecky
janekopecky@yahoo.com

No portion of this publication may be reproduced, reprinted, or otherwise copied for distribution purposes without express written permission of the author and publisher..

**DEDICATED TO**

**all Historical Society Members who spend countless hours volunteering to preserve history.**

## ACKNOWLEDGMENTS

I wish to acknowledge the following people and organizations for their contributions to this book:

My husband, John, for his support and encouragement

My daughter, Susanne, for endless hours of editing pictures

Teresa Sherman-Jones for the initial editing and assistance in organizing the book

Tyler Tichelaar for his expertise in the final editing

Stacey Willey of Globe Printing for her guidance and getting the book into publication

Bill Nesbit for collecting old Gould City photos and Bill Ehn for putting them on disks

John Blanchard and the Newtown Township Historical Society

Barbara Powell for sharing the Heinz Family Photo Album

Marilyn Fischer and the Gulliver Historical Society

James Weber and Carmeuse Lime & Stone of Gulliver, MI

Caroline Diem and the *Newberry News*

*The Manistique Pioneer Tribune*

The Soo Line Historical Society

Amber Ackley-Olsen, William Gillette, Gordon and Janet Hamill, David LaRose, Doug Nelson, Lucille Kenyon, Arbutus Snyder, Jerry Mattson, Elaine Webber, Rhonda Clark, Arvella Gorsche, Lawrence and Raymond Heminger, Paul & Janet Heinz, Bill and Donna Morden, The Bowman Family, The Salvino Family for sharing their family stories and photographs.

# TABLE OF CONTENTS

Preface ............................................. 6
PART ONE: HUNTSPUR'S BEGINNINGS ................. 9
   INTRODUCTION ................................. 10
   QUARTER PICTURE OF HUNTSPUR ................. 12
   HOW HUNTSPUR GOT ON THE MAP ................. 14
   THE FRANK HEINZ LUMBER COMPANY .............. 20
PART TWO: INTERVIEWS ............................. 25
   MABEL BAUERS ................................. 26
   LEON HEINZ: 1980 ............................. 37
   VANATTA BROTHERS ............................. 45
   BILL MORDEN .................................. 47
   LEOLA GILROY TENNYSON ENGLES ................ 51
   INLAND LIME AND STONE COMPANY ............... 57
   THE GREEN SCHOOL ............................. 63
   VERNON LANSING GOUDREAU ..................... 71
   SEUL CHOIX POINTE LIGHTHOUSE AND MUSEUM .. 76
   HAROLD BOWMAN ............................... 77
   BERNICE ACKLEY .............................. 89
   FLORENCE HEMINGER ........................... 91
   VERNON (MICK) LEE ........................... 93
   KENNY LEE ................................... 112
   WESS EMERY .................................. 118
   JUDGE QUINLAN ............................... 124
PART THREE: THE CICERO CONNECTION .............. 129
   JOE KOPECKY ................................. 130
   BLANCHE KOPECKY ............................. 138
   CONCLUSION .................................. 142
   About the Author ............................ 143

## PREFACE

In 1979, I had completed all requirements for a master's degree in elementary education with the exception of four elective credit hours. I'm a local history buff so I suggested to my advisor that an oral history practicum would be a good fit for me. She agreed.

Even as a young child, I enjoyed hearing elderly family members and neighbors talk about what life was like growing up. Their stories fascinated me, and I asked many questions, probably to the point of being a bit nosey, but they usually answered with an interesting story.

Time moved on. Many of the people I had visited as a child passed away. I became involved with activities that keep young people occupied, and then I moved into adult life, but my interest in history never waned. Now, in 1979, I was back doing what I loved—interviewing family members and neighbors—but this time, I was armed with a tape recorder, a notebook, and some knowledge on how to conduct a proper interview.

When my oral history practicum was completed, I packed all the taped interviews in a box and stored them in the back of my closet. I felt many of the interviews did not meet the professional standards required by my professor, so I did not submit them to the university, but I did not dispose of them, fortunately. I kept my tape recorder handy, and on occasion, continued interviewing.

In 2011, a notice in the *Advisor*, a local weekly advertising paper, published in Manistique, Michigan caught my attention, "Meeting of Newton Township Historical Society, Gould City Township Hall." Newton Township is in Mackinac County in the Upper Peninsula of Michigan and close to my home.

I attended that meeting of the recently formed historical society, and as a result, I discovered that because of my 1979 and 1980 taped interviews, I had the only known history of Huntspur. Therefore, I volunteered to write the history of Huntspur, a logging town in the Upper Peninsula of Michigan, from its beginning in 1871, to its end in 1929, when Inland Steel Company of Chicago bought the entire town and surrounding properties for its new limestone quarrying operations.

So, thirty-three years after storing my tapes, I retrieved them from the back of my closet to begin transcribing. I immediately learned that audio tapes deteriorate over time. I lost a few minutes of my first interview when the tape recorder ate the tape. I didn't want to risk losing any of my other interviews so I brought them to the audio visual department at Bay De Noc Community College, Escanaba, MI, where John Anderson did an outstanding job of transferring them onto CDs.

My original intent was to write only the history of Huntspur, but as I continued transcribing my tapes, I realized the book should expand beyond Huntspur. *Huntspur and Along the Tracks* is a book about a piece of Michigan history that no one knows about. True stories of the rise and fall of Upper Peninsula timber towns are told by the people who lived in them. The stories move from Huntspur along the railroad tracks to nearby towns and through time into the Great Depression. They depict a way of life that may shock some people. They give the reader insight into a timber-town economy, the harsh conditions the residents survived, and the local culture. They tell the tales of murder, theft, infidelity, tragedy, love, and life in an era when advanced law enforcement and modern medicine did not exist. Survival was contingent upon hard work, strong will, perseverance, and good luck.

While most of the tales are from Michigan's Upper Peninsula, I have included two recorded stories from Chicago, Illinois during the Al Capone era that follow the book's theme. These true stories are told from the perspectives of people who lived there and were trusted by "the mob."

The interviewees have all since passed away. Their stories are interesting, engaging, well-told, and deserve to live on. We can learn much from our past when we take the time to listen to those who came before us.

I have been honest to the interviews but have made some necessary alterations. Any grammatical or usage errors are left in order to stay true to the voice of the interviewee. The names of several people were not clear on the tape recorder so I spelled them phonetically.

## PART ONE: HUNTSPUR'S BEGINNINGS

## INTRODUCTION

Prior to railroads, logging camps were located near water where logs could be dumped, then floated down rivers to mills. The Industrial Revolution of the late 1700s into the 1800s spurred the development of power-driven machinery, creating a demand for iron and coal and faster transportation. The Great Chicago Fire of 1871 as well as changing lifestyles created a new demand for construction and lumber, which in turn led to a new demand for labor. Thousands of immigrants came to America to work and find a better life. Because of railroads, vast areas of interior virgin forests were now able to be logged. Huntspur began as one of those lumber camps.

According to Larry Easton, Soo Line Historical Society member, the first train came through Huntspur the first week of January, 1887. There are no records documenting how it got its name. It was a common practice for railroad crews to name new spurs for identification purposes so they often chose the name of a fellow railroad worker and combined it with spur. In early school board records, Huntspur is spelled as two words (Hunt Spur). Later, when the post office began, on October 9, 1889, it became one word and the official post office stamp was Huntspur.

*Quarter Picture of Huntspur: Following are three close-up details of scenes in it.*

## QUARTER PICTURE OF HUNTSPUR
### Described by Leon Heinz
### c. 1900 (Courtesy of Leon Heinz Collection)

This is a picture of one-quarter of the town of Huntspur. Old time cameras could not take a panoramic picture, so traveling photographers would take four pictures of a town that would later be put together.

*QP people dressed up*

It was a big event when photographers came. Everyone came dressed in his or her best clothes. My parents lived in the little house next to the false front hotel. My sister gave me this picture five years ago (1975) and said, "Look at big me in this picture."

*The store*

The store is next to the Soo Line. A twenty-four foot platform connects the tracks to the store. You can see a crane that was used to hang the mail bag on. The mailman riding the train put a hook out and caught the mail bag, hauled it into the mail car, and sorted the mail while the train was running. You can see a packet of shingles after they were sawed and packed for shipping. You can also see small wooden cars that ran on this railroad. Only the corner of the school I went to is visible. My brother Frank's farm is just out of sight on the picture. He cleared and farmed three hundred to four hundred acres.

*Fenced in yard*

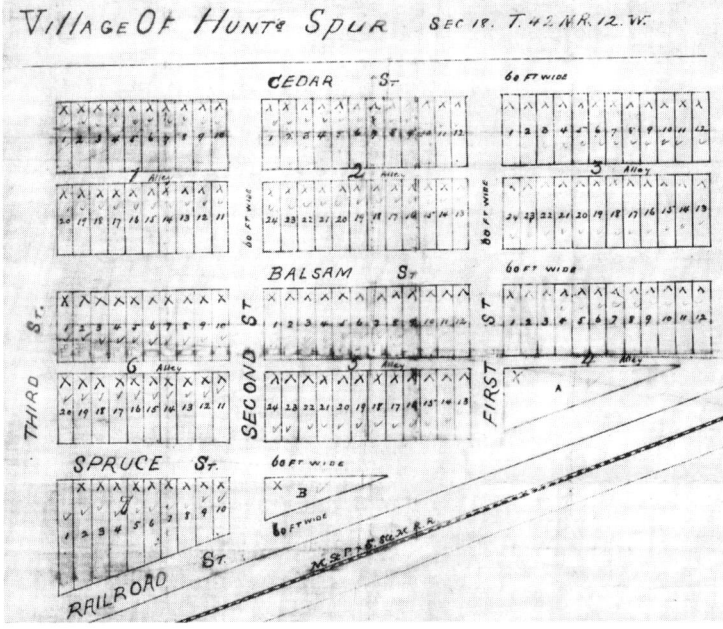

*1892 Village of Huntspur Plat Map (Courtesy of James Weber)*

## HOW HUNTSPUR GOT ON THE MAP
### TRANSCRIBED FROM LEON HEINZ NOTES
Written for Jane Kopecky

March 2, 1980

Huntspur got on the map because it was a lumbering and mill town. Shortly after the railroad was built, the Pankratz Brothers moved in and started the first logging company and built and operated a large steam mill that sawed white pine and hemlock into lumber, made cedar shingles, and made hemlock lathe for plaster in houses. They also built and operated two other shingle mills.

All these products were shipped by the Soo Line. Two small railroads [spurs] hauled timber from the woods to the mills. These railroads were standard gauge, but the steel rails were lightweight. The steam locomotives and *Russell Rail Road* cars were also lightweight. The cars each had two bunks.

Men and horses were located in the woods, and in the winter, the logs were hauled by teams of horses and oxen on four runner sleighs to the landings. The landings were located near the spur where the logs were loaded onto the railroad cars. Each car hauled one tier of sixteen-foot logs.

Huntspur was built on the north and south sides of the Soo Line. The large store next to the track store sold hardware, groceries, men's and ladies' shoes—a near complete stock. A warehouse was built next to the store. The store was operated for many years by the Upper Peninsula Cedar Company.

The company built a large bunkhouse and a square-front hotel to house 200 or more woods and mill workers. They also built fifty family houses. These houses were cheap [to] put up. They had cedar shingles and cedar siding. Cattle and pigs ran loose, and gardens and houses were fenced to keep them out.

A good-sized one-room schoolhouse was built that held seventy-five kids. First through eighth grades were taught there. There was also a large dance and amusement hall. Occasionally, men arrived on the Soo Line with muzzled large brown bears who performed.

The big steam mill burned down completely in 1903 and was never rebuilt. There was lots of virgin cedar left and the cedar shingle mills operated for many years after. But the white pine and hemlock were getting thinned out and there wasn't a market demand for hardwood such as maple, yellow birch, and beach so the big logging companies left—a lucky turn of events for my brother Frank.

*Pankratz House c. 1900 (Courtesy of Leon Heinz)*

*Huntspur logging camp men (Courtesy of Heinz Family collection)*

*Huntspur cook camp c. 1890. (Courtesy of Heinz Family collection)*

*Grandma Heinz holding baby at Stack Lumber Co., others not known c. 1900 (Courtesy of Heinz Family collection)*

*Huntspur c.1910 Men taking a break (Courtesy of Heinz Family Collection)*

18 ~ *Huntspur and Along the Tracks*

*1926 "Mrs. Snyder's Hungry Five" L to R: Bernice, Leo, Dorothy, Vernon, Bobby in front. She had two other children Lawrence (Sweed) and Eileen after this picture was taken. All of her children were two years apart in age.*

Mrs. Evelyn (Michaels) Snyder died at an early age. The younger children were farmed out to various orphanages. Bernice married, Bruce Stewart not too long after at age 17. They moved to Whitedale (Gulliver) and lived on a farm. Bernice located her younger siblings and brought them to live with her. The older children helped out at the Heinz Camp, as did the younger as they got older. Arbutus Snyder, wife of Leo said, "Frank Heinz took them under his wings. He was good to them."

*1942 Bernice (Snyder) Stewart at Heinz camp in Huntspur with her children L to R: Richmond (Dick), James, Willard (Wid). She was pregnant with her youngest, Sharon, at the time the picture was taken.*

2-8-20

Clifford,
    Hope you enjoy the book about Huntspur. I contacted the author Jane Kopecky who is wintering in Arizona and she told me they were being sold at a gift shop in Manistique which is where I got a copy for you. I don't know when you're birthday is, but consider this your birthday present.
    Some day I plan to write the Weber Family History. I have gathered several old photos and newspaper clippings over the years. If there is a photo of your Dad + Mom and all your brothers and sisters, maybe you could bring it on your next visit and I would like to copy it.

Cousin Jim Weber
ph 906-450-8131

*Huntspur 1934*

The house closest on right was the William (Chum) and Florence Heminger home. Behind it is the Mr. and Mrs. LaPine home. Mrs. LaPine was a teacher. Several other houses are behind them. The schoolhouse has four windows and is the furthest back on the right. The big building left, in back, is the hay barn. Others, unknown. (Courtesy of Heminger Family collection)

## THE FRANK HEINZ LUMBER COMPANY
### Transcribed from Leon Heinz notes
### Written for Jane Kopecky

Frank started The Frank Heinz Lumber Company. He had a few camps, men, and horses in the area as new markets were created; hardwood flooring, hardwood furniture, spruce, and balsam pulpwood cut into eight-foot lengths, cedar poles of assorted lengths; railroad ties, which were hand-hewn with a broad axe in the woods, and cedar were in demand.

His company grew. The Heinz workers lived in large camps. He also bought timber from a number of independent lumberjacks living in cabins who cut scattered areas. There were no trucks or tractors in those days. All the wood was moved by horses and four runner sleighs and shipped on the Soo Line.

About 1928, Inland Lime and Stone Company was buying limestone acreage so Frank Heinz Lumber Co. sold Huntspur and the surrounding area to the Inland. At this time, Heinz Lumber had three camps left: one in the Green School, one at Parkington, and the other in the Dolomite area near Seul Choix Point.

In addition to horses, Heinz Lumber now had a fleet of trucks, trailers, tractors, and bulldozers in use. Stumpage was getting thin in some areas, so in 1939 he moved his equipment eight miles north of Chatham, Michigan near the Rock River. The company had one mill at that location that cut hardwood lumber, cedar lumber, and hardwood railroad ties. It trucked logs to Rapid River and Wells and Cedar to Menominee.

In 1942, Heinz Lumber Company moved camps, equipment, portable camps, and about ten teams of heavy horses from Chatham to Ross Creek, north of Seney. It also had three mills at Cusino, near Shingleton, where it shipped finished products by railroad.

In 1949, the camps, equipment, horses, trucks, and tractors were sold. The lumber and logging was at an end for Heinz Lumber Company.

*1930 Frank Heinz Residence (Courtesy of Heinz Family collection)*

*c. 1910 Frank Heinz on left second row, first on left, with arrow pointing toward him. (Courtesy of Heinz Family collection)*

*Frank Heinz Horse c. 1940 - Draft horses skidded the logs from the woods to the truck. (Courtesy of Heinz Family collection)*

*Frank Heinz Truck 1940*

*L to R: William Gardner, camp foreman; Clifford Terrian, log scaler; next two men not known; Leon Heinz, equipment mechanics; Louis Ray, truck driver.*

*Description supplied by unknown newspaper clipping. (Courtesy of Heinz Family collection)*

*Cook Camp Women c.1900*
*L to R: Mrs. Snyder, Theresa Heinz, Bula ? (Courtesy of Heinz Family collection)*

*Chatham Heinz Camp 1940. Bobby Snyder with load of logs. (Courtesy of Heinz Family collection)*

24 ~ *Huntspur and Along the Tracks*

*Heinz Cook Camp. Not known (Courtesy of Heinz Family collection)*

*Five Heinz Brothers and year born*
*Back: Frank 1892    Michael 1894    William 1907*
*Front: Leon 1904    Adam 1900*
*(Courtesy of Heinz Family collection*)

# PART TWO: INTERVIEWS

*Three Baby Sisters L to R: Mabel, Lula, Evelyn (Elsie) Clement (Courtesy of Heinz Family Collection)*

## MABEL BAUERS
### Jane Kopecky Interview 1980

My name is Mabel Bessy [Elizabeth] Clement Bauers. I was born January 1, 1891, in Fargo, North Dakota. I'm eighty-nine years old. I was very young when we moved to Huntspur. My sister Lulu was a baby. She couldn't walk yet and there's not two years between us.

Cows roamed and ate grass wherever they could and our gardens had to be fenced in. Strawberries were bigger and blackberries and raspberries grew next to our house. There were flowing wells, lots of horses, and lots of people got killed by the train.

### ABANDONED

When we moved to Huntspur, things were going good. We were friends with the Pankratz. They had a big yard and their daughter, Marie, and I played together. My mother was also friends with Mrs. Addatt. Their family owned the Addatt Hotel and Saloon and they took in boarders. Cassie Addatt and her older sister were teachers who lived in Gridley just a few miles down the track toward Blaney Junction.

My mother was a seamstress and took in boarders and my dad worked in the woods and helped Mother when he could. My parents hired a newly-arrived girl from Sweden to help at the boarding house. My dad, Otto Clement, paid special attention to this girl and evidently fell in love with her. They left one day on the train together to get supplies in Manistique but didn't return. A sheriff caught them in Wisconsin and Dad was arrested for abandoning the family. He was sent to the Waupun Prison in Wisconsin. In those days, you went to prison for abandoning your family.

Dad kept writing Mother, telling her he had changed. He told her he loved her and would be a good husband. He then asked her if she would write to the authorities and tell them she needed his help to support her and the three little girls. Mother wrote the necessary letters and Dad came home.

He was a good boy for a while. Though I was very young, I still remember the day he left. He was dressed in his best clothes and Mother helped him put in his French cuffs that he was so proud of. He looked so handsome. She waved to him as he got onto the train and that was the end. No one ever saw him again.

In those days, people didn't travel far so it was easy to disappear. We heard rumors that he was somewhere on the West Coast in Washington, but we never did know for sure. He left us in Huntspur to survive on our own. Mother continued boarding people and sewing. My sisters and I took on more responsibility to help her and support ourselves. A few years later, Mother married Mr. Olsen, one of our boarders. He was a good husband and kind to me and my sisters.

## CLEANING OUT THE BARS

Down the tracks toward Seul Choix was Finn Town. The Finns worked mainly as shingle weavers. They made and sold whiskey and were terrible drinkers. When they got drunk, they fought amongst themselves or with anyone else. I was afraid to walk past their camp.

Lumberjacks from French Town stole some of the Finns homemade whiskey. When the Finns discovered what happened, they walked to French Town to fight the lumberjacks, but they had gone to the saloons in Huntspur. The Finns went after them.

Beside the tracks were two saloons next to each other. The Finns went into the first bar and found some Frenchmen. They had a terrible fight. They smashed everything. Then they went into the second bar and fought and smashed everything in there. I looked inside the next morning and broken glass was everywhere and lots of blood. It was a mess, but nobody was killed.

## MURDER IN HUNTSPUR

Two mornings later, the train stopped on the hill and the engineer blew the whistle. This was unusual so the town folks rushed out to find out what was happening. The train had stopped before running over a dead man lying on the tracks. Mother told us the fresh snow was covered with blood. They followed the blood trail to the steps of a saloon where they found a bloody board. The man had been murdered, beaten to death. His body was dragged onto the tracks to make it look like a train death. No one would tell who killed him. There wasn't an investigation; we didn't have police.

The murdered man was a Finn who had walked to town alone for supplies. He had a wife and six children in the old country, and he was saving his money to bring them here. He had nothing to do with the fights or smashing of the bars.

Years later, on his deathbed, Ty Richards, a single bookkeeper, confessed that he had killed the Finn. Mr. Richards ate with us at my mother's boarding house. He was a quiet man, a nice man who was kind to us. Sometimes when I went to the store, he would give me a ride home on the handlebars of his bike. I thought that was so much fun. He ate right under our roof and we never suspected. He just didn't seem like the type.

### MRS. KNOPH GETS KISSED

Mrs. Knoph was a Bohemian widow whose husband was killed on the railroad tracks when walking from Gridley Junction. She barely spoke English and was a little odd. She had a beautiful cabbage patch and was known for making sauerkraut. She had a lot of kids and she would make the kids get into the wooden barrels with their bare feet to stomp the cabbage down.

The whole town thought they'd have a little fun. They told one of the town drunks who cleaned spittoons in saloons to kiss Mrs. Knoph. Mrs. Knoph was raking up cabbage in her garden. The garden was fenced in to keep the cows out. The drunk walked over to her place with all the people following. He went into the garden and chased her around until he caught her and then tried to kiss her. The people were hollering and laughing. Finally, Mrs. Knoph yelled to her son Jimmy to get the axe and hit the drunk with it. That ended everything. He stopped. It was just like a scene from *Little House on the Prairie*.

### UNUSUAL DEATHS

It was not unusual for people to get run over by a train.

We got our mail twice a day by train. A crane on the platform hooked the mail bag from the train. Paul Brushy said, "I'll get the mail." We heard the train whistle blow. He went running across the tracks and was killed by the train. I was there to get the night mail and I had to step over his body. I was so scared. It was horrible to see.

Another time, a white man married a colored woman and they had two boys. They had a nice house and a flowing well. The wife left him and he started drinking. He was killed by a train coming from the junction [Blaney]. He was drunk. After he died, the woman came and got the boys. I heard one of them got killed in World War I.

"Calspar" was a camp a short ways from Huntspur. A big mean man lived there. Nobody could lick him. He was in love with some woman who left him and he lost his mind. He wasn't seen for a long time and nobody bothered to look for him. It was winter and he went out into the woods in his stocking feet. They found him dead in a brush pile.

### DANGER IN THE STREET

The company horse barn was not far away. When it got hot, the horse flies bit the pastured horses so they'd run into the barn to escape the flies. Mother did the laundry outside on the porch with a washboard. One summer, she gave me five cents and told me to take Lulu to the store to buy soap. We were walking in the street when the horses came running toward us to get into the barn. I ran one way and Lulu ran the other. A horse knocked Lulu down and stepped on the side of her head. I hollered to a man to help, but he just stood there. Mother ran into the street, picked Lulu up, and carried her to the house. Her face was badly bruised. There were no doctors. Mother kept her in a chair and she got better.

I was very little when I saw a drunk man, a bully, picking on a small man. He pushed the man's head into a horse watering trough to drown him. He kept pushing his head down. No one came to help until he was almost dead. Finally, someone stopped it. I couldn't get over it. I thought someone should have helped him sooner.

Steal—a lot of stealing went on. We had a big gobbler. Someone stole him. Some other kids and I were walking along the train tracks and when we looked inside the empty box car, we saw our dead turkey. They didn't even eat it.

### ENTERTAINMENT AND DAILY LIFE

We fished by the little creek. We used a bent common pin for a fishhook and caught all the trout we wanted. We helped Mother can venison and vegetables. We played baseball, Hide-and-Seek, and "Doc on the Rock." There were two teams, each team having a big rock. On top of the big rock, we'd place little rocks. We threw stones to knock little rocks off the big rock. The winner was the team that knocked the most stones down.

We had a lot of socials at the big dance hall across from the school. Everyone brought food to eat and we'd visit and play. Every Saturday, we had a dance. Someone played the violin, organ, or other instrument. We had masquerades. I was twelve or thirteen when I masked.

On Sundays, we did a lot of walking. We walked down the railroad tracks or wherever there was a road or path. Sometimes a minister came from Manistique to hold church at the school or someone's house. I went to every church gathering.

We didn't have a cemetery. Funerals were held in houses and the bodies buried in Gould City or Manistique.

I attended the one-room school on the hill across the street from the dance hall. In the morning, we sang as we marched around the room, carrying our knapsacks. When it was my grade's time for instruction, the teacher called us to the front of the room. We worked arithmetic on the board and were taught penmanship, reading, geography, and history. When you completed the eighth grade, you could teach school.

My eighth grade teacher was David Hern. He used to bother me. He stood by me while I was doing my lessons. It looked like he was trying to make a date with me. He asked me all kinds of questions. Years later, when I was married and had a baby, I went to a ballgame in Curtis. I was sitting in our first car, a Ford, an open car. By gosh, he found me and started talking about old times. He owned a little store in Curtis and was married with children.

## MEMORIES OF EAST LAKE

My sisters and I were small when stepdad worked at "East Lake Camp" one summer. When we boarded the train, my mother carried her bird in a cage and my sisters and I each had a kitten.

This was a big camp with lots of lumberjacks. Some men lived in the bunkhouse, and many of the families lived in small houses nearby. We lived in one of the small houses.

## "HE STOOD IN THE STREET AND CRIED AND CRIED"

On payment day, the workers went to the office to pick up their payslips that told them how much money they had earned, and then they would take the slips to headquarters to get paid. A Polish man, who couldn't speak English, picked up his payslip and the bookkeeper said, "Don't open that envelope until you get to headquarters or you won't get paid." The man didn't understand what he said so he stood on the steps and opened the envelope and the bookkeeper came out and took the envelope. The man didn't get paid. He stood in the street and cried and cried. That was so mean. I felt sorry for him.

## ROBBERIES

Jim Robinson and Slim Jim were two men who robbed, sometimes stealing from the rich and giving to the poor. Slim Jim was fond of the cook's wife, Mrs. Bredler. He'd steal clothes for her. One day, Slim Jim came through the woods carrying a stolen ham. He tried to give it to Mother, but she wouldn't take it. He gave it to a Polish family who didn't speak English.

A lot of peddlers came through. One day, a peddler came with a big pack on his back. He went to the camp and the men took everything he had. They wouldn't pay him for it, and they were going to beat him up. He came running to our house for safety.

One day, Dad was working in the woods and Mom was at the spring getting water. Us kids were alone in the house. Slim Jim rode his horse halfway into our house. We hid our suitcase under the bed where he couldn't find it. We were so scared. Dad came home and was he mad.

Mom had a jewelry box with her watch, my dad's gold watch, lockets, and a charm from the old country, and some money. One day, Mr. Bredler came to our house and asked if he could buy the watch for his wife. Ma said no. A few days later, Mrs. Bredler asked Mom to help her bake pies. Us kids were out back picking blueberries. While we were gone, Mr. Bredler came and stole everything. Us kids had our own money in saving banks and he even took that. We felt bad.

When we returned to Huntspur, I had to go to La Croix's house on an errand and Mrs. Bredler was there visiting. She was wearing my mother's ring, and I recognized the watch with the chain. I told my parents, but we didn't do anything. There was nobody to report it to.

## *Escanaba Daily Press* June 21, 1988
### Mrs. William (Mabel B.) Bauers

MANISTIQUE—Mrs. William (Mabel B.) Bauers, 97, Manistique, died at 9:23 p.m., Saturday, June 18, at the Schoolcraft Medical Care Facility where she had been a resident.

She was born Jan. 1, 1891, in Fargo, N.D. She spent the greater part of her life in Hunt- Spur, Mich., she resided at Blaney Park and later moved to Gulliver. She attended Hunts Spur Public School as a young girl.

The former Mabel B. Clemet married William F. Bauers July 2, 1908, in Manistique. She was a member of the Infant of Prague Church in Gulliver.

She was preceded in death by her husband, William, May 10, 1955, a daughter, Mrs. William (Virginia) Willour, July 30, 1982, and a son, Russell Bauers in 1925.

Survivors include: one son, William R. Bauers, Saginaw; four daughters, Mrs. Jack (Evelyn) Rodgers, Gulliver, Mrs. Eleanor Brown and Mrs. Peter (Arvella) Gorsche, Manistique, and Mrs. Marvin (Peggy) Anderson, Grand Rapids; 16 grandchildren; 43 great-grandchildren; 14 great-great-grandchildren; several nieces and nephews.

Friends may call at Messier-Broullire Funeral Home, Manistique, beginning at 4:30 p.m. today. Parish liturgical prayers will be held at 8 tonight at the funeral home. Funeral services will be held at 10 a.m. Tuesday at St. Francis De Sales Church, Manistique, with Rev. James Menapace officiating. Burial will be in Fairview Cemetery, Manistique.

*Three Adult Sisters: Mabel, Lula, Elsie (Courtesy of Heinz Family Collection)*

*1904 L to R: Francis and Adam Bauers, Theresa Heinz with children. L to R: Francis, Michael, Helen (being held), Frank (Courtesy of Heinz Family Collection)*

*Mabel and Elsie with Lee, Elsie's son (Courtesy of Heinz Family Collection)*

*Bill Bauers sitting on chair, Mabel on his left. Other members of the family not known. (Courtesy of Heinz Family Collection)*

*Anton and Anna Bauers, parents of Bill Bauers (Courtesy of Barbara Powell, Heinz Family Collection)*

*Bear Hunting.*
*Bill Bauers, second from left (Courtesy of Heinz Family Collection)*

*LaCroix's Bar c.1900*
*(Courtesy of Heinz Family Collection)*

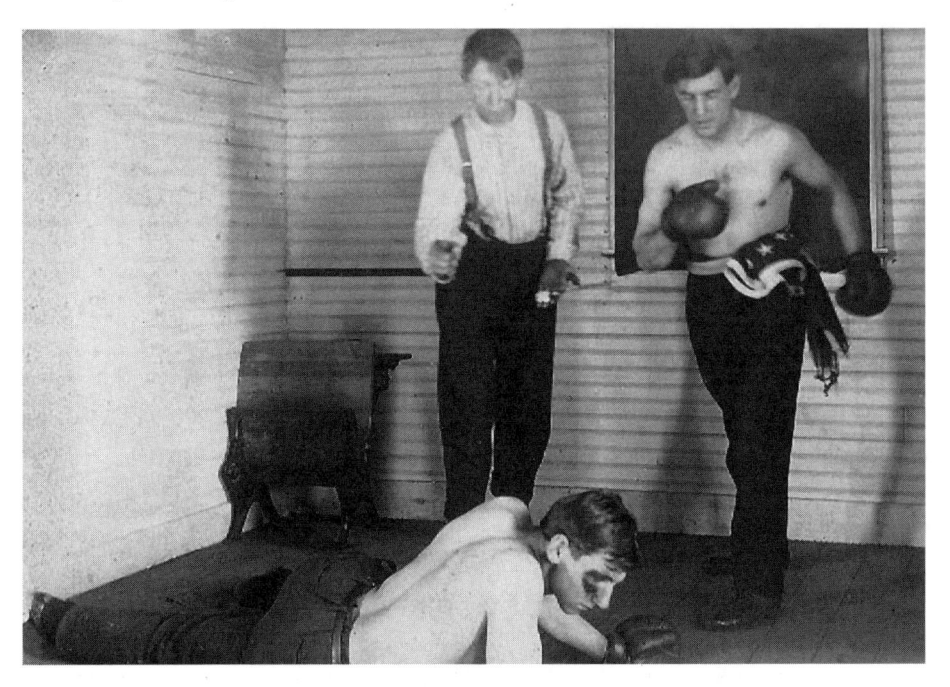

*c. 1910 Boxing at the Huntspur School*

*Frank Heinz, Charles Swayers (down), Unknown LaCroix boy counting
(Courtesy of Heinz Family collection)*

## LEON HEINZ: 1980

I was a firecracker baby. I was born on July 4th, 1904 in Schoolcraft County, three quarters of a mile from the Mackinac County line where Huntspur was located.

Huntspur will always be my first home. I have good memories. That's where I was born and raised. I have a jeep and I ride there often and remember where all the old houses were and where everything was.

When my parents arrived in Huntspur it was already built. My folks came from Germany where dad was a blacksmith, mechanic, and mason. He could figure out how to do anything.

Immediately after getting off the train, my parents moved into that little house by the hotel. It later burned. The next day, Dad got a job in a mill at Gridley. My mother packed a pail for him and he hiked one and a half miles down the tracks to work. He couldn't speak a word English. Imagine that.

Pankratz Brothers big steam mill burned in 1903, the year before I was born but I know this just as if I were there because my folks talked about it. After the little house burned my folks got an 80 acre farm about three quarters of a mile from Huntspur just across the county line. My brother Bill and myself were born on that farm, delivered by midwives.

It was real primitive. There were lots of deer and bear. When we were kids we'd walk along the Milakokia River in bear tracks and then they'd walk in our tracks. We never thought anything of that. One evening we were looking out the north living room window when we saw a big bear standing on his hind legs looking at the pigpen. I wasn't afraid so I said to my mother, "Let me shoot him." Everyone at that time had a pile of guns in the house.

She was better thinking than I was. She said, "If you shoot him and wound him he'll come after us."

When I attended school there were between forty-five and fifty students. Many families had left when the big steam mill burned. It was never rebuilt. The white pine and hemlock were thinned out but some logging was still going on. Plenty of virgin cedar was standing and the cedar mills operated strong until the lands were sold to Inland Lime and Stone Company and everyone had to move out.

When the Finns, who cut cord wood, and the mill crews got together drinking in one of the three or four saloons they would fight. Very seldom anyone got murdered but there was a Sears and Roebuck catalogue printer from Chicago who retired here because of his health. He moved his family into a log house in the woods. They found him dead and suspected he might have been knocked off. My sister later moved into that house.

When I was twelve years old, I worked. I was a big boy. During summers when we weren't in school, there was always work to do. I helped cut hay, milk cows, grow potatoes and other food, and cut wood for our own need. We were never bored. The people living in Huntspur never had to cut stove wood. The cedar mill had a team of horses and a two-bit box cart, a cart with wooden sides, and if you needed wood, the company delivered it to your house for no charge.

Railroads were necessary to ship the wood products, bring in supplies and transport people. The first automobile didn't come into Huntspur until about 1917 so people walked or rode the train. Groceries came in by rail and were unloaded on the platform by the store. You had to go to the company store to get them. It was like the store people talk about with the old pot belly stove, post office, and a family living upstairs. In those days, sugar was three cents a pound, a suit for an eight-year-old boy $2.50, and a good pair of shoes for a man $2.00. The company ran the store until the Stites family from Traverse City bought it and ran it.

There were two trains, a 10 and a 5, that carried passengers and mail. One went east at 10 o'clock in the morning toward Gould City and then at 5 o'clock it went west to Manistique. It was pretty handy. The fare to Manistique was 35 cents. We didn't ride it often because money was scarce, but when we did go to Manistique, we rode in on the 5, stayed overnight, and came back on the 10. We stayed at the American House. My folks and us kids ate a lot of good meals there for 35 cents apiece. I remember seeing the Park Hotel, the Osse, and the Hiawatha Motel by the Soo Line Depot, all gone now.

## BASEBALL

Baseball games were played on Sundays. My older brothers played on the Lakeshore Stars Baseball Team. They played against teams from Blaney, High Island, and Beaver Island. When they played against Blaney, they used the railroad pede[1] and hand-pumped it the five or six miles to Blaney. If they couldn't get a peed, they walked. They'd play ball, hang around a while, and then come home. When they played against the island teams, they walked to the beach and boated over. The Israelites lived on High Island. They didn't believe in cutting their hair; it hung past their shoulders, but they were good ball players.

The old times are gone. People hiked, rode a train, or hopped a train. Polly Lavake lived at Seul Choix Point and hiked along the shore to Manistique to buy Christmas toys, then hiked back the next day carrying them in a bag on his back. That was the only way to go. There wasn't a road.

Automobiles changed everything. I saw my first car, a *Model T*, at Blaney in 1916 when I was twelve years old. It was backing up and turning around and the first thing I thought was, "Boy, do they make a lot of noise." Back in those days, you could hear the timing gears. They didn't have helical gears. They had straight tooth gears. You could hear a 1920 *Chevrolet* car coming from two miles on a quiet evening.

Tires were no good at that time and cars weren't much better. If you got 5,000 miles on a tire, they put it in the window at the First National Bank in Manistique. If a car had 5,000 miles, you'd see a blue fog coming out behind it. They didn't make glass enclosed cars until 1924.

I helped build the road from Huntspur to the Greenschool when I was just a kid. It was all done with horses. It used to be a two rutted outfit. You could figure that in the fall or spring you'd get stuck going one way or the other. Coming in or going out.

Sometime in the late 1920s, an Indian family lived near Huntspur. Their young child died during the winter. Because the roads were not plowed, they could not give the child a proper burial. They wrapped him in blankets and buried him in the snow bank to preserve his body. I had a car, and when the roads cleared that spring, I brought the family and the baby's

---

[1] Velocipede- A four wheeled, hand powered vehicle used by railroad workers to inspect and repair rails. They were stored next to the railroad tracks in a shed and were light enough to be carried by two men. They were often used by local people for transportation.

body to Nahma for a proper Indian burial at the Indian cemetery.

I saw many things come into fashion. In Huntspur, we had a crank record player. The first time I heard a radio I was at the Knights of Columbus Hall in Manistique. They had head phones and only one person could listen at a time. Later they came out with a horn and we could all listen.

*Jacob and Theresa Heinz with children, Frank, Francis in back, and Michael and Helen in front (Courtesy of Heinz Family collection)*

*The Manistique Pioneer-Tribune* August 7, 1997

### Leon J. Heinz

MANISTIQUE—Leon J. Heinz, 93, of 537 Part Ave., Manistique, died Thursday, July 31, 1997, at Schoolcraft Medical Care Facility, Manistique.

He was born July 4, 1904, in Huntspur, Mich., the son of Jacob and Theresa (Knight) Heinz. He attended school in Huntspur and graduated from Sweeney Automotive School, Kansas City, Kansas. He spent the greater part of his life in the Manistique and Gulliver areas.

On Aug. 17, 1939, he married Mary Louise Rubick in Manistique. She died on June 26, 1959.

He was a member of St. Francis de Sales Catholic Church, Manistique; Manistique Knights of Columbus Council 2026 and United Steelworkers of America Local 4302. He retired from Inland Lime and Stone, Co. in 1969.

Survivors include: one son, Paul (Janet), Manistique; four grand-daughters and 12 great-grandchildren.

In addition to his wife and parents, he was preceded in death by four brothers,

Frank, Michael, Adam and William; two sisters, Frances Bauer and Helen Heinz; and a great-granddaughter, Jodie Rivard.

Visitation is from 4 to 7 p.m. on Saturday at Messier-Broullire Funeral Home. Services will follow at 7 p.m. with Rev. George Gustafson officiating. Burial will be in Fairview Cemetery, Manistique.

*Huntspur, 1932 Theresa Heinz with daughter Helen in front of family house (Courtesy of Heinz Family collection)*

*c. 1920 Frank Heinz Family on pede (Courtesy of Heinz Family collection)*

42 ~ *Huntspur and Along the Tracks*

*Baseball team on its way to a Sunday game. Believed to be a Manistique ball team. (Courtesy of John Blanchard, Newton Township Historical Society)*

*Huntspur and Gould City, MI Ball players (Courtesy of John Blanchard, Newton Township Historical Society)*

Jane Kopecky ~ 43

*Blaney, MI Baseball Team Russell Bauers, Bill Heinz, and Bill Bauers on right rear. (Courtesy of Heinz Family collection)*

*Leo Heinz car at Heinz lumber camp. (Courtesy of Heinz Family collection)*

*Leon Heinz, car enthusiast, standing in front of his 1927 Essex Super Six car. Photo taken in Manistique. (Courtesy of Leon Heinz collection)*

## VANATTA BROTHERS
### Leon Heinz Tells About the Vanatta Brothers

Aaron and Winsel Vanatta owned and operated a big steam mill in Huntspur. They also had a cedar, shingle, and log mill on the shore of Lake Michigan in the bay west of Hughes Point. People once referred to it as Vanatta's Bay. Fishing was a big industry along the north shore and the Vanattas made boxes for shipping the fish. They also made their own boats and put their own engines in. Those were primitive days. They took those boats across Lake Michigan to Hart and Evert where they bought fruit. They peddled it along the shore from Menominee to the Soo. The Vanattas also made wooden boats to ship wood. In 1917-1918, I loaded lots of pulpwood onto those boats at Seul Choix.

*c. 1910 Huntspur, Vanatta Shingle Mill (Courtesy of Heinz Family collection)*

*c. 1910 Huntspur, Vanatta Mill (Courtesy of Heinz Family collection)*

*c. 1910 Vanatta Mill on shore of Lake Michigan. (Courtesy of Heinz Family collection)*

## BILL MORDEN
### April 8, 1980

My memories of Huntspur are mostly of hard work and desperate times.

I was born in Lake City, Michigan, on May 24th, 1910. Our family moved to Huntspur when I was a young boy because my dad got a job as a caretaker at the Nicholes Farm. Today you would call it a hobby farm. It wasn't much of anything. It was a cattle ranch. Nicholes let the cattle run all over the woods, and pretty soon, there were no cattle. People ate them up.

When I was fourteen years old, I worked for the Adam Heinz General Store delivering groceries to logging camps with one horse and a dray on winter roads. The roads were packed, not plowed. Heinz supplied groceries to his camps and other logging camps in the area. I delivered every Saturday and sometimes after school and once in a while on Sundays. Saturdays I might make two deliveries. I went by myself but often gave people rides to a camp or to Huntspur to catch the train. Sometimes I didn't get home until after midnight. If I was really tired on the return back, I'd tie the reins, cover up with a blanket, and sleep. Prince, the horse, knew his way home and he'd walk at a steady gate until he got close to the barn; then he'd start to run. That woke me up.

I got paid two dollars a day, but if I delivered groceries past Porcupine Crossing, I got four dollars a trip. The furthest camp I delivered to was Batty Doe Lake Camp, about five miles, and the next furthest were the Bill Bolenga and Wood Camps. The Buckeye Camp was the biggest camp with its own railroad spur. The next biggest camp was the A.D. LaCroix Camp. There were several other smaller camps, but I can't remember their names.

A lot of families moved in from Kentucky. They were rough. They'd get drinking and sometimes there was a stabbing. Some of them came to Huntspur hoping to hide away. Every so often, the sheriff would come and take one of them out because of something they did back home. They lived in tents and cut cordwood.

They came in the spring and stayed right through the winter in those tents. They banked the tents with snow and heated with a wood stove. A young pretty girl about twelve years old died of pneumonia. Spen Johnson and I came out to get the body and bring it out on a dray. When we went inside, we saw there was no floor and it was cold and damp.

In 1924, Inland Lime and Stone Company sent four miners from Wakefield, Michigan to sink a test hole to evaluate the rock. They boarded at our house.

They dug the test hole by hand with shovels. They put the stone in buckets and my dad and Bill Bauers winched it to the surface by hand. The test hole diameter was big enough for the men to work inside it. After the hole got too deep, I think the depth was forty feet, they got Frank Heinz's tractor to pull the buckets up. They worked on the hole for a couple of months around the clock in two twelve-hour shifts. It was hard physical work.

They loaded the stone onto a dray by hand and took it to what is now Co. Road 433. This is where they removed the stone from the dray and loaded it onto a truck to be hauled to Calspar to be tested. Calspar is where they did all the research work.

When Inland Lime bought the land, all the buildings had to be torn down or moved out. Frank Larson tore down and moved the Frank Heinz house to the Lakeside area in Manistique and turned it into a duplex. Dad tore down the old store and rebuilt it on Gulliver Lake next to where Gerard Heinz lived. It's the cottage Judy and Jim Rogers lived in before they moved.

Many of the cedar houses were moved and are still standing. People in Green School, Gulliver, Gould City, and other towns live in them.

There weren't any hard feelings about having to move out of Huntspur because the Inland provided work and a paycheck.

As you drive along Batty Lake Road today, the store was on the left-hand side along the track. Frank Heinz lived on the right-hand side where the lilac bushes are. I guess the old chimney is still standing. Up on the hill, Adam Heinz had a nice house. Across from the school was the Stites Farm. The Vanatta Brothers had a little mill that made fish boxes. Alvin Goudreau owned the general store and post office and Adam Heinz bought it from him. Other family names I remember are Charlie Swayer, Charlie Poker, Ben Lockwood, and Hider.

## The Manistique Pioneer-Tribune August 8, 1996
### William E. Morden

William E. Morden, 86, died August 1, 1996 at his residence.

He was born May 24, 1910 in Falmouth, MI, son of the late William W. and Bertha (Udell) Morden. He moved to Manistique at the age of six. He attended Huntspur and Manistique Area Schools.

On February 27, 1935 he married the former Blanche E. Hulshof in Manistique.

He was a member of the First United Methodist Church in Manistique, the United Brotherhood of Carpenters and Joiners of America. He was employed as a carpenter, working for various companies until his retirement in 1972. He enjoyed wood carving, hunting and fishing.

Survivors include: his wife, Blanche E. of Manistique; two sons, William E. (Donna) Morden of Coeur d'Alene, Idaho and Michael L. (Linda) Morden of Manistique; one daughter, Margo Gleason of Lake St. Louis, MO; two sisters, Viola Salter and Hazel Hastings, both of Manistique; six grandchildren, seven great-grandchildren and several nieces and nephews.

In addition to his parents, he was preceded in death by three sisters Lola Keelean, Ruby Hastings and Elizabeth Hamill.

Visitation and funeral services were held on August 5 at the Messier-Broullire Funeral Home in Manistique. Rev. Raymond Wightman officiated at the services. Burial was in Lakeview Cemetery in Manistique.

*1916. Bill Morden with sister Lizzy. (Courtesy of Morden Family collection)*

## CALSPAR

Calspar was the site of a small quarry near Huntspur owned by the White Marble Lime Company. Large kilns burned limestone into lime. Inland Steel Company bought the property from White Marble Lime sometime in the late 1920s or early 1930s. Tests of the stone showed the Dolomite limestone and High Calcium (HI-Cal) limestone in this area have superior chemical characteristics that make it highly valuable for a variety of industrial purposes.

*White Marble Lime Company known as Calspar installation*

Inland Steel Company vacated the Calspar Quarry about 1935 and began its new quarry about two miles away. The houses were moved out, many to the Green School Location and Gulliver. The quarry hole filled with water, covering the abandoned kilns. It became a favorite swimming hole and party place for local youths. About 2000 the area was barricaded and closed to the public.

## LEOLA GILROY TENNYSON ENGLES
### March 5, 1980

Dad was a foreman and troubleshooter for White Marble Lime Company. White Marble was owned by the Nickerson Family and run by George and Ken Nickerson. White Marble owned the Blaney Quarry, known today as Calspar. The name was changed to Calspar because there were places nearby also named Blaney; the Blaney Junction, the Blaney Grade, and Blaney Park. It was confusing. The employees at the quarry changed the name to Calspar-cal for calcium and spar in place of spur because they thought it sounded better. Western Lime's kilns turned limestone into lime. Later Inland Steel built a laboratory to test stone [for industrial purposes].

My first memory of seeing the quarry was the summer 1911, when I was four years old. Dad was staying at the boarding house where he also had his office. Mother took us on the train to visit him. Besides the boarding house, there was a bunkhouse for the workers, a store operated by Jean and Jim Rodgers, three houses, two farms, and the kilns.

Our family moved to the Blaney Quarry from Manistique every summer so we could be near Dad. We lived in a log cabin a short distance from the quarry.

Within a few years, there was a post office in the store, with Jean Rodgers as postmistress, and eleven houses. Some of the houses were built on site and some square houses with cedar shingles were moved in from Blaney. The bunkhouse became a community building after the workers moved into the houses and there was a polling place to vote. A train took the stone out, and once a day, a peed took the mail and anyone who wanted to ride to the Blaney Junction.

We had many parties in the community building. Everyone brought a dish to pass and the Tennyson boys and Leo Willour played music. They were quite talented and played a variety of musical instruments: violin, guitar, banjo, Hawaiian guitar. Our teacher, Cecil Venus, would often walk from the Green School to stay at our house and attend the parties. When

I was fifteen years old, the town got a radio with an earphone that was kept in the community building. We sat in a circle around it and took turns listening.

We lived at Calspar every summer, then moved back to Manistique during the school year with the exception of my third grade, seventh grade, and eighth grade. My sisters and I walked two miles [one way] to the Green School. The year I was fourteen and in the eighth grade, we had an unusual amount of snow. The snow banks were so high you couldn't see the train; then the train and peed couldn't get through the snow and had to stop running. We walked to school on the hard, packed snow.

That April, the snow turned to slush. By the time we arrived at school, our snow pants, shoes, and boots were soaked and frozen. I got pneumonia and we couldn't get out to a doctor. The neighbors helped. They brought eggs and milk to make eggnog and cream for nourishment. They brought me wine for strength.

Because of the weather, only one boy, Joe Parker, who lived on one of the farms and was older, continued to walk to school. Because we missed school for four weeks, the teacher made a bad judgment call; she reported our absence to the school superintendent. The authorities summoned our parents to court for not sending us to school. Dad shut down the quarrying operation for two days. He took all the men to Manistique on the train for the hearing. Dad paid the bill for everyone's hotel room, supper, breakfast, and train ride. The judge dismissed the case and the county had to pay the expenses for the trip and furnish transportation for us to get to school for the rest of that year. Dick Carstenson drove us with a horse and light wagon.

The following fall, when school started, one of the houses that had been moved in from Blaney was turned into a two-room schoolhouse and we had our own teacher, Francis Jenks. The Spriners, Barbeaus, Benwells, and Parkers were some of the students.

*The Manistique Pioneer-Tribune* February 1996

### Leola E. Engel

Leola E. Engel, 88, of Manistique, died January 30, 1996 at the Schoolcraft Medical Care Facility in Manistique.

She was born July 6, 1907 in Manistique, daughter of James and Stella (Cutler) Gilroy. She graduated from Manistique High School. She spent the greater part of her life in Gulliver and returned to Manistique in 1985. She was a member of the Maplegrove Mennonite Church of Gulliver, the Schoolcraft County V.F.W. Auxiliary Post No. 4420 and the Addie Rebekah Lodge of Gould City. She was a former distributor of Stanley Products and a Foster Grandparent in the Manistique Area Schools.

On November 6, 1924 she married William E. Tennyson in Sault Ste. Marie, MI. He preceded her in death May 12, 1963. She married Kenneth E. Engel March 19, 1967 in Gulliver. He preceded her in death May 14, 1981.

Survivors include: three sons, William H. (Elly) Tennyson, James (Betty) Tennyson, both of Gulliver, Robert L. (Bonnie) Tennyson of Bossier City, LA; one daughter, Betty (Truman) Zook of Goshen, IN; two sisters, Vera Tennyson of Manistique and Florence (James) Manndia of Louisville, KY; 16 grandchildren, 35 great-grandchildren, 12 great-great grandchildren, several nieces and nephews.

She was also preceded in death by one brother, Howard Gilroy and two sisters; Lillian Lancour and Alva Stephenson.

Visitation and funeral services were held on February 3 at the Messier-Broullire Funeral Home. Rev. Jay Martin officiated at the services. Burial will be in the Fairview Cemetery in Manistique.

*Calspar General store c. 1910 (Courtesy Jean Rodgers collection)*

*Calspar boarding house c. 1910 (Courtesy Jean Rodgers collection)*

## GREATEST BLAST IN HISTORY

*THE MANISTIQUE PIONEER-TRIBUNE*

Thursday, March 17, 1932

Greatest Blast in History Shot by Inland Lime and Stone Co.

Half Million Pounds of Dynamite Used Blowing Large Area of Limestone

---

Government Officials Study Blast for Scientific Purposes; Shock Is Recorded at Washington

The greatest blast in the history of mining was shot off Wednesday afternoon at one and a half minutes after three o'clock at the limestone quarry of the Inland Lime and Stone Company, 22 miles from Manistique. Almost a half million pounds of dynamite were used in displacing a ledge of solid rock one mile long, 200 feet wide and 40 feet in depth.

Scientific study of the blast was made by government officials throughout the nation for the purpose of securing data that will be beneficial in recording earthquake shocks in the future. The explosion was recorded at Georgetown University at Washington, D.C., which is 1,500 miles distant.

The record, represented by a tiny wavy line, showed the shock was fainter than any earthquake, reported Father J. S. O'Connor, seismologist. The explosion made it possible to determine with great accuracy the speed of earthquake waves through rock, he explained, because the exact time of the blast and its distance from seismographs was known.

The big shot was made on a signal given from the naval observatory at Annapolis. The United States Coast and Geodetic Survey, Washington, was in charge of the radio hook-up at the quarry and the blast was shot when a signal from the naval observatory was received.

Those nearest to the scene of the blast felt very little shock and report only a muffled roar. The long stretch of rock heaved up in the center while steel casings and smaller pieces of rock were hurtled into the air at least five hundred feet. It was all a matter of history in the space of a few seconds, the entire charge seeming to explode at the same instant. However, the Associated Press reported that Professor Charles W. Chapman, of Michigan State College at East Lansing, recorded three distinct vibrations. The first was received 59.6 seconds after the explosion.

The explosion of a single cap set the big blast off. The charge to the 4,000 holes filled with dynamite was carried through seven miles of TNT fuse. The holes were about forty feet in depth. Seventy-five men were busy for eight days in loading the charge.

Perched high atop a specially erected scaffold on the roof of the power station were news reel cameramen. They were quite a distance from the blast but their position gave them an excellent view. Company officials and newspapermen were some 300 yards from the blast and used steel railroad cars for protection.

There was only one known casualty. One of the workmen picked up a small snowbird that evidently had a broken wing. The bird was taken into the power station and will be kept there in the hope that it may recover.

Manistique residents did not feel any shock from the blast. The shock evidently was felt more severely by persons about a half mile or mile away than it was by those close at hand, but even then it was only a slight tremor and no damage is reported.

The shooting of the big blast is bringing much publicity to Manistique. Newspapers all over the country are featuring the story. Movies will also be shown throughout the nation and it is expected that newspapers will also carry pictures.

*Building the Port Inland Dock c. 1930. The logs were cut, then towed to the harbor site by diesel tug. (Courtesy Leon Heinz collection)*

*Building the Inland Harbor Trestle c. 1930 (Leon Heinz collection)*

*Building Inland Harbor Trestle c. 1930 (Leon Heinz collection)*

# COMPANY HISTORY
## INLAND LIME AND STONE COMPANY

*Inland Lime and Stone Company circa 1940s. Photo Contributed by Paul Petoskey* Source: *Manistique Centennial Book,* 1960

"In 1928, the Manistique area received another industrial boost when Inland Steel Co. of Chicago began explorations and preliminary engineering for a limestone quarry and purchased the White Marble Lime Co. The firm built a railroad and harbor near Huntspur in 1929 and in 1930 the plant was built. The first car was dumped from the crusher on Oct. 6, 1930 and the first shipment of high quality limestone was made on the steamer Joseph Block, November 14, 1930.

Annual production has risen from one million tons in 1931 to over four million tons at present. The firm produces limestone for steelmaking, which accounts for over two-thirds of its production, and stone for aggregate, lime burning, cement, paper mills and agricultural limestone. The limestone is exceptionally pure, having an analysis of between 97 and 98 percent calcium carbonate.

58 ~ Huntspur and Along the Tracks

## 2012 CARMEUSE OPEN HOUSE BROCHURE

The following brochure was handed out when Carmeuse had an open house in 2012.

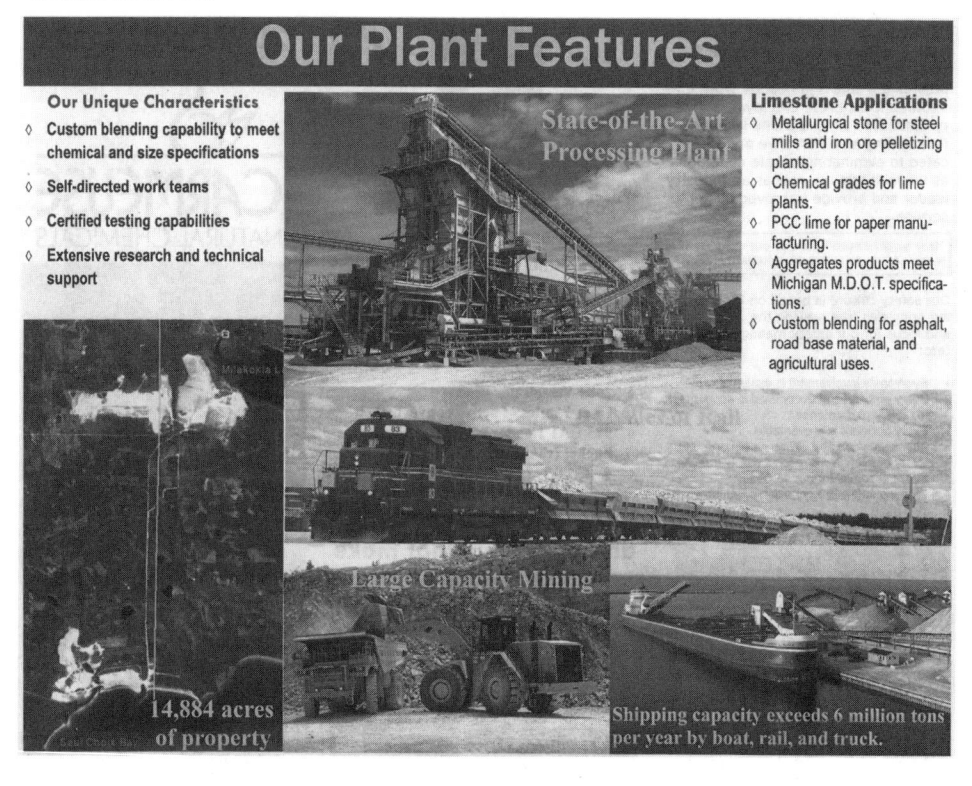

### Our Plant Features

**Our Unique Characteristics**
◊ Custom blending capability to meet chemical and size specifications
◊ Self-directed work teams
◊ Certified testing capabilities
◊ Extensive research and technical support

State-of-the-Art Processing Plant

**Limestone Applications**
◊ Metallurgical stone for steel mills and iron ore pelletizing plants.
◊ Chemical grades for lime plants.
◊ PCC lime for paper manufacturing.
◊ Aggregates products meet Michigan M.D.O.T. specifications.
◊ Custom blending for asphalt, road base material, and agricultural uses.

14,884 acres of property

Large Capacity Mining

Shipping capacity exceeds 6 million tons per year by boat, rail, and truck.

## Port Inland Fun Facts
◊ **Over 100 million tons of stone shipped since 1992.**
◊ **200+ Vessels per year.**
◊ **Over 7 miles of active conveyor belt.**
◊ **993 CAT Loader with 17 cubic yard bucket (each tire costs $40,000).**
◊ **4 - CAT 777 100 ton haul trucks.**

## SCHOOLCRAFT COUNTY LIMESTONE AND PORT INLAND HISTORY [2]

- White Marble Lime Co. – late 1800s-1930
- Inland Steel Co. – 1928-1989
- Pfizer Specialty Minerals – 1990-1992
- Mineral Technologies Inc. Speciality Minerals – 1992-1998
- Oglebay Norton Co. – 1998-2008
- Carmeuse North America – 2008 to present

\* \* \*

Regardless of the name of the company that owned the property, the local people usually refer to it as "The Quarry" or "Port Inland" or just "The Inland." It has had a positive economic impact on the area for over one hundred years. Many of its employees have family connections with original settlers of the area and work on the exact spot their ancestors once lived and worked.

---

[2] Courtesy of James Weber

*Chris Benish is the great-grandson of Mabel Bauers. He remembers her driving him to Huntspur and talking about living there.*

*Bill Parish on lunch break at Carmuese.*

*Gavin LaRose, employed by Kasbohn Drilling, a sub-contractor of Carmeuse. Gavin's great-grandfather, John LaRose, had a logging camp in Huntspur.*

*Mike Rosebush, one of five people from his family who have worked at "The Quarry."*

*Jim Weber, Carmeuse Production Manager. Jim's father, Matt Weber, worked for Schoolcraft County and drove one of the first snowplows into Huntspur in the late 1920s. he is 104 now, but he still remembers the Hotel, General Store, and Heinz's big house at Huntspur. The foundation, flowing well, and stone fireplace are still there.*

## THE GREEN SCHOOL

If you travel west along US 2 about seventy miles from the Mackinac Bridge, you'll come to County Road 433. Turn left (East). The Green School began at the intersection of US 2 and County Road 433 and extended to Vanatta Road, a distance of about one-tenth of a mile. If you continue east along 433 for two miles, you'd be near Calspar, and if you continued five miles farther, you'd arrive at the gate of Carmeuse properties, the present day quarry, and near Batty Doe Lake Road, the road to old Huntspur.

The Green School is a place in Mueller Township, Schoolcraft County, named after a bright green school. In the early 1900s, the area was referred to as Maple Grove because of its beautiful maple forests. Neither Maple Grove nor Green School ever had an official recorded name.

Before Huntspur and Calspar closed, Maple Grove consisted of the green school, Pete Olson's store, and a few families. As automobiles became more common, travelers used the brightly painted cedar shake "green school" as a US 2 landmark. The Green School became a place.

In the 1930s, as residents had to leave the property purchased by Inland Steel, the area's population grew. Two schools were needed to house the influx of students. The school from Huntspur was moved and placed beside the green school. A.D. LaCroix left Huntspur and built a tavern at the intersection of US 2 and County Road 433. Aaron and Winsel Vanatta moved their mill a half mile from the school to what today is Vanatta Road. Families moved their houses from Huntspur closer to the green school. It was a convenient short drive to their new jobs at Inland Steel.

Across the street from the green school, on the southeast corner of the intersection of Vanatta Road and highway 433, was Pete Olson's store and gas station. It became a popular stopping place. Travelers would stop for gas, buy ice cream cones, use the outhouse, and feed Pete's pet bear. Pete often entertained people by wrestling with the bear. For a few cents he offered a drink of whiskey from an unwashed shot glass he kept by his cash

64 ~ *Huntspur and Along the Tracks*

register and he bartered for goods, legal or illegal. He was quite a character and anyone who knew him had a "Pete" story to tell.

*Maple Grove Gas Station (Courtesy of William Gillette collection)*

Maple Grove Inn
Peter C. Olsen, Proprietor
(Grandpa)

Purchased: 1928
Sold: May 24, 1964

Green School,
Gulliver, Michigan

"Little Billie Gillette"
Student and
Grandson

*Maple Grove Inn (Large picture)*

*Maple Grove Inn. (Courtesy of William Gillette collection)*

*GS store close up.*

*Girl & Bear (Courtesy of William Gillette collection)*

*Bear & German Shepard (Courtesy of William Gillette collection)*

*Pete Olson (Courtesy of William Gillette collection)*

*Maude & Pete (Courtesy of William Gillette collection)*

*Green School kids c. 1934 William Gillette first row on left; Alveta Terrian, back row second from right, others not known (Courtesy of William Gillette collection)*

*1943 green school boys - (Courtesty of the Freeland family)*

*Green Schoolhouse moved c.1950. A new school was built and the old "Green School" was sold and moved one half mile away to its present site. It was renovated and is now the home of Janet and Gorden Hamill.*

\* \* \*

*Mueller Township Hall. The population of the Green School area has declined. The schools, Pete's store, and LaCroix's Bar are gone. The water pipes of the town hall are drained during the winter, the heat is shut off, and the building is closed until warm weather arrives.*

*The fire department was disbanded. The fire trucks and fire fighting equipment are gone. There were not enough young people to meet the requirements for a fire department. A room in the back of the building is used during the winter for township meetings and as a polling place.*

## VERNON LANSING GOUDREAU
### 3/12/1980
Interview at Goudreau home on Seul Choix Point

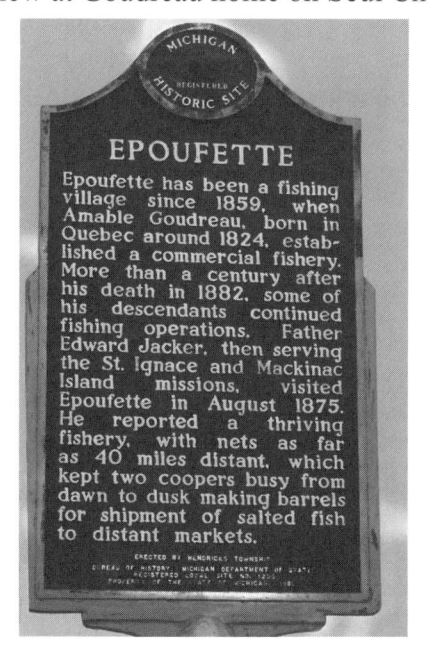

> **EPOUFETTE**
>
> Epoufette has been a fishing village since 1859, when Amable Goudreau, born in Quebec around 1824, established a commercial fishery. More than a century after his death in 1882, some of his descendants continued fishing operations. Father Edward Jacker, then serving the St. Ignace and Mackinac Island missions, visited Epoufette in August 1875. He reported a thriving fishery, with nets as far as 40 miles distant, which kept two coopers busy from dawn to dusk making barrels for shipment of salted fish to distant markets.

*Epoufette plaque (Courtesy of Gulliver Historical Society)*

My family had been fishermen for generations. I started fishing when I was a very young boy and I've always lived on the Point. When I got older and got a job at Inland Lime and Stone Company I fished on my days off, on weekends, and during vacations.

Fish were plentiful so we didn't have to go out far into the lake. We'd be gone two to two-and-a-half hours unless we were delayed by weather. When we got back, we packed the fish for shipping. Fishing is different today; gill nets are outlawed.

Dad placed the first nets in these waters. My grandparents were fishermen from Epoufette who owned land on Seul Choix Point. In 1871, when my dad, Amable Orville Goudreau, was sixteen years old, Grandfather sent him here in a boat with a small crew to scout the area for fishing. He sailed back to Epoufette and reported to Grandfather that he thought this was a good fishing spot.

He returned to Seul Choix to be in charge of five different fishing rigs: four gill net rigs and one pond net rig and about twenty men. Each rig required three to four men. He brought a cooper to make barrels for shipping fish. The barrels were made of pine and pine trees were plentiful here. One cooper could make one or two kegs a day.

At that time, the beach was the highway. There were no roads, no railroads, and no farmers. There was no navigation light or lighthouse. There may have been a few people living on the bay side of the point, but I don't know of anyone living on the west side. Manistique had only three buildings—two log buildings and one frame building. One of the buildings belonged to Booth Fisheries.

Dad rowed out daily to check for fish. One day, he rowed out and saw whitefish, schools of them. He told the crew to set the pond net stakes and bring out the nets. The crew said he'd get a "bawling out" because it was too early in the year to start fishing. The nets weren't to be set until fall. He said, "I'm the boss now and we'll set the stakes."

They caught so many fish they couldn't leave the nets in. They had to keep pulling them. They filled all the barrels and ran out of salt. Dad left after dark, alone, on his sailboat for Epoufette to get more supplies. He arrived at Grandfather's in the middle of the night during a terrible storm. He woke Grandfather. When Grandfather saw him, he was upset. He thought a tragedy must have happened for him to be out so late in such weather.

Dad returned to Seul Choix the following day with a barge carrying one ton of salt and barrels. Grandfather said, "I guess from now on you're the boss." Dad always had charge after that.

The crew pulled the nets out of the water by hand; there weren't any net lifters. They used floating stones (stones tied to the bottom of the net) to keep the bottom of the net down and cedar or pine poles on the top to keep it up. Today, they use lead on the bottom and cork, aluminum, or plastic on the top.

At that time, fish were salted with brine, packed in one-hundred-pound barrels and freighted by schooners that arrived maybe once a month, sometimes more often. The schooners went wherever there were fishermen. They went to the islands and along the shores buying fish that they sold mainly in Chicago. They made a business of that. That's how fish got sold years ago. The schooner had a store above that sold supplies, even stoves. It was a floating store.

Men walked along the beach looking for work. Years ago, if you left one place of work to go to another, it didn't mean you weren't satisfied or a good worker. Men liked to move around. They'd leave after season and maybe return in the winter to tell Grandfather they'd be back to fish or they'd stay and cut timber. Sometimes they'd catch fish under the ice crown at the straights [of Mackinac]. One man worked for my dad for seventeen years, which was unusual.

Dad and Uncle Alex freighted fresh fish to Manistique with a sailboat. Then they bought the first gasoline-powered boat on the point, The Harvey G. It was a Burger Boat built by Henry Burger in Manitowoc, Wisconsin with a Columberg Engine from Two Rivers, Wisconsin. Burgers are in their third or fourth generation of boat-building and are known throughout the United States. They still build ocean-going yachts. (The Harvey G. compass is on view at the Seul Choix Light House.)

John Coffey had the three nicest tug boats on the Great Lakes; the Berger, the Alice, and the Annabelle. He and Dad were good friends and he hauled lumber from Manistique for building our house and Uncle Alex's.

Dad told us about a terrible accident. A neighbor by the name of Gotking had a good-sized sawmill near the mouth of the Milakokia River where he cut pine trees into lumber with a gang saw. Some of the dock pilings are still standing. Gotking was short on labor one summer so Dad helped him out. Gotking accidently cut himself with the saw, a big gash down his belly. They waited for the train to arrive [at Gulliver depot], then took him to Manistique where he died a few hours later.

### INDIANS

This Point has always been a fishing village. Before my dad came, there were about 400 Indians. They seined for Whitefish at Seiner's Point. Most of them died of smallpox and are buried here.

Indian Peter John Beaver split rails for my grandfather when my dad was a little boy. After Ella and I got married, he worked for Dad repairing twine and cutting poles for the pond nets. During the winter, he went to Canada. He was known as an Indian doctor. He used all kinds of herbs for medicine. He'd come to the door and beg for a potato or a piece of salt pork, but he never stole anything. He was a quiet man and a good man. When he died in Manistique, they stated his age as ninety. There was some kind of mistake about his age because he had to have been about 115.

Most of the Indians were good. A lot of people had them wrong. I was around them a lot when I was young. There were 450 living on High Island. High Island was supposed to be reserved for the Indians. John Thomas was their chief. There were no police and they never had trouble. They had dances once a week, and even if they were drinking, there weren't fights. The only fights were just fun wrestling. They had a good time.

They had a nice church and a public school. The school was in operation until about 1936. Their teacher was a smart girl, a nice girl from Cross Village, and my brother used to write to her. She was part Indian. She taught both English and Indian. The Indians were hard to teach because they didn't care to go to school.

When the fishing yield dropped in the 1930s, the Indians left High Island. Many moved to Beaver Island and some moved to Chicago to work on tugs, not fishing boats. They started with the water and stayed with the water.

## THE ISRAELITES

Late one night, after I'd gone to sleep, the Israelites knocked on our door. It was storming and Dad told them to come into the house to sleep. I was very young. I woke up early because there was more activity than usual. I walked into the kitchen and saw a group of men with beards and long hair. They combed and braided their hair, then crossed it around their head. I'd never seen men with long hair. At first, I was scared; then I thought, "Boy would I like to cut that hair off." They ate breakfast and were very clean and polite.

We called them Israelites. They lived on High Island and belonged to a religious group called the House of David. They didn't allow members to cut their hair, use alcohol or tobacco, and they didn't eat meat.

If you landed on their dock, they came out to help. They built a lumber mill, but it wasn't successful. They did have a successful bakery shop that sold really good bread and rolls. Sometimes they'd land in our harbor in a small twenty-seven-foot tug to pick berries. They had a big passenger boat too, but the captain wasn't an Israelite. They were good ball players. They played against teams from Beaver Island and Benton Harbor; sometimes they played against the Indians. Once in awhile, the Israelites or Indians came here to play against local teams. When games were played, the whole community came to watch.

*House of David Baseball (Courtesy of Gulliver Historical Society)*

## The Manistique Pioneer-Tribune June 12, 1980
### Vern L. Goudreau

Mr. Vern L. Goudreau, 74, of Seul Choix Point, died June 4, 1980, at 10:30 p.m. at Little Traverse Hospital in Petoskey, Mich.

He was born March 20, 1906, in Seul Choix Point and attended the Seul Choix and Manistique Schools and was a member of the Divine Infant of Prague Catholic Church of Gulliver and the Inland Lime and Stone Company 25 Year Club. Mr. Goudreau was employed by the Inland Lime and Stone Company as a dredge operator and service truck driver for 26 years until his retirement April 1, 1971.

He was married to the former Ella King at Manistique on January 27, 1923.

He is survived by his wife, Ella, of Seul Choix Point; four sons, Gregory, James, Amable and Robert Goudreau of Gulliver; two daughters, Mrs. Emeric (Theresia) Bosanic of Manistique, Mrs. Victor (Verna) Hellebuyck of Essexville, Mich., one sister, Mrs. Wilfred (Lenore) Fish of Manistique; 21 grandchildren; 29 great-grandchildren and several nieces and nephews.

He was preceded in death by his parents and grandson, Stephen Goudreau.

Friends called at the Messier-Broullire Funeral Home beginning at 4:30 p.m. on Friday, June 6.

Liturgical prayers were said at the funeral home at 7 p.m. and K of C rosary was said at 8 p.m.

Complete funeral services were held at St. Francis de Sales Church at 10 a.m. with Father Darryl Pepin officiating.

Pallbearers were grandsons, William Goudreau, Albert Goudreau, Duane Hellebuyck, Emeric Bosanic Jr., Dennis Goudreau and Ronald Goudreau. Burial was at the Fairview Cemetery.

## SEUL CHOIX POINTE LIGHTHOUSE AND MUSEUM

*Seul Choix Lighthouse (Description and photo courtesy of Gulliver Historical Society)*

   Seul Choix Pointe is located in the northwest corner of Lake Michigan in Schoolcraft County, Michigan. The station was established in 1892 with a temporary light, and this light started service in 1895, and was fully automated in 1972. It is an active aid to navigation. There is now a museum at the light and both the building and the grounds are open for visitors from Memorial Day until mid-October.

## HAROLD BOWMAN

I was born 1902 in Gould City, Michigan. When I was three years old, my parents separated and Mother took me with her to Port Arthur, Ontario where her brother, Jack Taylor, operated several logging camps. Uncle Jack met us at the train depot in Port Arthur; then we traveled to his camp by dog team and sleigh. That spring, Mother got a job cooking on train. She couldn't keep me with her so, for a small fee, she arranged for me to board with the Davis family in Bemidji, Minnesota. They had several children of their own.

I stayed there more than a year when the money stopped coming and we lost all contact with Mother. My welcome at the Davis house had run out. I was left to run on my own, finding food and a place to sleep wherever I could. When mealtime came, I ate at the home of whomever I happened to be playing with. When night came, they gave me a bed. I remember being hungry. If any food was left unattended, I ate it. I'd steal an apple or any food I could find.

I don't remember the details, but I was told that Mother's sister, Mary, came to Bemidji to find me. She contacted Grandpa Bowman, informing him of my whereabouts and situation. Grandpa wired the local police department to find me and put me on a train to Gould City.

I remember the day the sheriff found me in a general store. I was about to grab some food from a bin when he walked over to me. I thought he'd come to put me in jail. He asked my name, then took me to the police station and fed me a good meal. They made a cot for me to sleep on until my transportation could be arranged.

The train ride to Gould City required a twelve-hour layover in Minneapolis. I was told to stay in the station, but I saw a woman carrying a lunch basket. I followed her outside. She sat on a park bench and began to eat. I sat next to her and she offered me part of her sandwich, which I eagerly accepted. I missed my train. A railroad official found me on street and escorted me to the depot.

Grandpa was in a state of panic when the train arrived in Gould City without me. Mr. Engel, the station agent, wired the terminal in Minneapolis and found out what had happened.

When I arrived in Gould City, Grandpa carried me and my old straw suitcase to a buggy and we left for home. Grandma ran out to greet me. She lifted me from the wagon and hugged me. We went inside where she fed me, then took off my clothes, handed them to Grandpa, and ordered him to burn them and my suitcase. She then gave me a bath in kerosene to kill the lice.

My grandparents were kind and loving and this was the beginning of my new life.

Shortly after my arrival, I got the measles. Because my body was in a run-down condition, I then got pneumonia. I was sick for eight months and so weak I couldn't walk. Grandma did her daily errands around town wheeling me in a baby carriage. My strength returned with loving care, Castor Oil, and a slew of homemade remedies.

Grandpa had a withered right hand. He came from southern Michigan where he had a farm accident involving a threshing machine with a big steam engine. His hand got crushed when he tried to grab a belt that had jumped off its rollers. In spite of the crippled hand, he was noted for his beautiful penmanship.

After the accident, he and Grandma moved to Gould City and started a livery stable business. Every spring, he bought a carload of Western Broncos; then farmers came in and they'd horse trade. He always kept fourteen for the livery barn and seldom let them out to anyone. Only Grandpa, an uncle, or someone Grandpa trusted was allowed to drive them for fear they wouldn't be handled right. He didn't want them to get sweaty, then stand in cold.

I liked being with Grandpa in the stable. Before and after school, I shoveled manure, curried and brushed horses, and oiled harnesses. A highlight of my week was Saturday when I went to the woods to work with Uncle John. I carried a lunch pail just like he did. We would build a bonfire at noon to thaw out our frozen sandwiches.

One of Grandma's fall duties was ordering supplies for the winter from the Sears and Roebuck Catalogue. It was an enormous catalogue. They sold groceries, clothes, harnesses, sewing machines; just about anything you'd want, all delivered by freight train. She and Grandpa sat at the table and wrote the order for our winter staples—salt, sugar, and dried fruit and whatever else they needed. They also bought supplies at Healey's General Store in town. I remember big barrels of corned and salted meat that we pulled out with a hook. A broad axe was left on the counter to cut cheese. Candy was displayed in wooden pails.

## SCHOOL DAYS

I attended the two-room school in Gould City where the county garage sits today. Dave Hearn taught the upper grades and Carrie McFadden taught the younger students. I walked past the back steps of McArthur's Saloon and Healey's Store every morning.

A cold north wind was blowing one morning as I walked to school. I pulled my mackinaw up around my head and kept my face down out of the wind. It was just breaking day when I got to the back steps of McArthur's Saloon. Jack Kempf was sitting on the steps in his shirt sleeves. I thought he must be crazy for being out dressed like that. I got closer and saw he was dead. He got drunk and froze to death.

Henry and Harvey May, from May's Hotel, were my best friends. We got into a lot of trouble. One day, Harvey and I were acting foolish and got a laughing streak. We had to stay after school. Miss McFadden said, "You boys like to laugh so much come up here and see how long you can laugh." She let the girls stay and watch. She had us sit in the front of the room with our hands on the desk. In the beginning, it was easy to laugh; after a while, it wasn't. Harvey stopped first. Every time we stopped, she hit us with a pipe on the thigh. The girls were laughing; they thought it was funny.

One morning, I killed a skunk and put it in a school vent. We didn't have school long that day; the kids were turned loose. I had to take the skunk out and stay after school for several days but the smell lingered.

Because I lived in town, I was the school janitor. I got paid a little bit; can't remember how much. In the morning, I filled the big wood stove at the back of the room so it'd be warm when the teacher and kids came; then I swept the floor. Anytime I got into trouble, I'd get my revenge. More than once, I'd pour pepper on the floor and make sure I was still sweeping when the kids came in. They'd sneeze.

During deer season, Grandpa made sure he had enough horses and buggies or sleighs, depending on the weather, to take deer hunters to and from camp. In those days, hunters arrived by train and depended on our livery. Grandpa trusted Harvey with his horses, and on this particular day, Harvey decided to skip school to take some hunters to Norton's Resort on the South Lake. He was twelve years old. They stopped along the way to buy whiskey and must have had a good time sharing it with Harvey because he returned to school totally sloshed.

Just after lunch, I saw Harvey tying the horse and buggy outside the school. I walked out to greet him. He was staggering and smelled of whiskey. I told him he shouldn't go inside. He said, "I'll be all right," so I helped him in. He fell asleep at his desk. I thought he should leave. Our seats were in the back row so it was easy for me to sneak him out. A ladder was propped against the outside of the school to gain entrance to the attic. My plan was to put him up there by the warm chimney to sleep it off. I helped him up the ladder and pushed him into the attic. I would have helped him across the lath and plaster ceiling, but I wanted to get back inside before the teacher noticed I was gone. I was walking in the door when lath, plaster dust, and Harvey fell into the classroom. I grabbed my books and lit out because I knew I'd get kicked out anyway. I took the horse and buggy home. Harvey had to get himself out.

Mr. Perkins, a fisherman from Scott's Point, got a group of us young boys to play ball against the Israelites on High Island. He took us over on his tug. The Israelites were strictly vegetarians and had hair halfway down their backs. They looked strange but were nice. They took us to the church to eat. Harvey, said, "Hell of a place to eat lunch; not a piece of meat in the whole place." They were good baseball players and I believe some went into big leagues.

Years later, I was working for Ford Motor Company and taking a correspondence course. I sent my homework to Chicago for correcting and grades. One day a paper came back and on the bottom was written, "Are you the same Harold Bowman who went to school in Gould City?" It was Miss Carrie McFadden.

## JUDGE HEALEY

Jim Healey was a bachelor from Ireland. He was the justice of the peace and everybody called him Judge Healey. The judge had the store and his brother had a farm on South Gould City Road where rocks are piled into fence lines. I spent a lot of time with the Judge. He had a little library in the back of the store and in the evenings he'd explain things to me. He let me read all the books I wanted. His nieces, Cassie and May, stayed with him when he got older and took care of him until he died; then they ran the store for many years.

Every morning on my walk to school, I passed Judge Healey's about the time he'd be looking at his thermometer. He had the unusual habit of lifting his shirt to compare the outside temperature with the air on his bare belly. One morning, it was warm and I rubbed ice on the thermometer to lower the temperature. He lifted his shirt and said, "Gee's, it's cold out today." The next morning, it was colder than hell so I lit a match and held it under the thermometer. The Judge came out, looked at the thermometer, raised his shirt, and said, "Gee's, it's warm out today."

## AROUND TOWN

In those days, many people were superstitious. They didn't like going near graveyards.

Bill Lyman had an old car with carbide lights. He strapped a carbide tank on the running board to make gas for the lights. He connected them with a rubber hose. It never did work very good. Bill and Joe Paluette were on a ride one night when the lights went out. Bill got out, shook the tank and put water in it, but it still didn't work. He kicked it off the running board and threw it into the graveyard.

Charlie Baker had a few old time superstitions stuck in his head. A few nights later, he was returning home from visiting the Leveilles. It was cold and raining so he pulled his coat up around his neck to stay warm as the team trotted along. Meanwhile, the rain had absorbed into the carbide, and just as Charlie was passing the graveyard gate, the place exploded. He just about killed his team getting back to Gould City. The horses were lathered up and Charlie made a big commotion. He told everybody a ball of fire flew out of the graveyard. He said hell was popping out. He was scared. Finally, someone went down there and found out what really happened.

Harry Salters had a lath mill with a swing saw. Hughie McLeon was working the saw when a crooked stick bound the saw and pushed it to the side. It sliced Hughie in the belly. He grabbed himself to hold his insides in. He walked across the tracks to the depot and waited for the train. He died in Manistique a short time later.

Scott's Point was quite a fishing town. They had a boarding house and their own baseball team. During the winter some of fishermen rented houses with an attic in Gould City where they stretched nets, repaired nets or made nets.

South of Gould City was Simmons Woods, owned by Simmons Lumber Company. It was an operating lumber town with a railroad. When I was thirteen or fourteen, we'd walk there on Saturday night for dances, then walk back home about four o'clock in the morning. Every town had a baseball team, but the Simmons hired a special train coach to carry their team to Manistique and along the tracks to other towns. They had some fancy players too.

## BRYAN

When I was little, I often stayed with Uncle Al at Bryan, a lumber town a short distance from Gould City, owned by Stack Lumber Company. It had an office, a roundhouse, a big steam loader, two steam engines, and a grocery store. Quite a few people lived there. Uncle Al ran the steam loader and my dad ran a steam engine.

Stack was a wealthy lumber baron who owned thousands of acres of land. He came here from Ireland, a poor immigrant. He owned a saloon in Escanaba and worked twenty-four hours every day. He slept on a chair tilted against the door at night so he'd wake up if someone wanted to come in. He didn't want to miss a customer. He wanted people to know they had a place to drink any time.

At that time, you could file for a Stone and Timber Claim from the government. It was like a homestead claim, only you didn't have to live on the property. He'd send lumberjacks out to find forty acres and sign for the claim. They'd bring it back to him and he paid them in whiskey for the claim. Most of the lumberjacks couldn't write; they signed with an X.

## LEAVING HOME

Upon the advice of a geologist, Mr. Gero and several other men from Manistique formed a syndicate to buy oil leases on Seul Choix Point. They hired a drilling company from Detroit, but so much scalping was going on they didn't trust them. They knew I had worked with Grandpa on his well-drilling rig so they encouraged the company to hire me. I was their "inside man." I was seventeen years old.

I began as a helper changing bits, splicing cable, and dressing 1,100-pound bits swinging a sixteen-pound sludge hammer. We didn't work shifts; we called them towers: two men on a tower. The afternoon tower started at noon and ended at midnight. The morning tower was from midnight to noon. We hadn't heard of the eight-hour work day yet. There were no unions, no strikes, no vacation pay, no overtime and you never missed a day of work.

We drilled two test holes. The first was 1,711 feet and took over one year to drill. We were capable of drilling 200 feet a day, but money problems delayed us. The syndicate would run out of money so we'd shut down the rig; then they'd sell more stock to get money and we'd start drilling again. Sometimes we were forced to shut down for repairs. We had more shut-down time than drilling time, but we got paid whether we worked or not. I suppose it was a good job for those days, but it was a lot of messing.

The second hole was drilled where Vern Goudreau lives now. It went 1,275 feet. There was no indication of oil, only shale. That ended the job at Seul Choix.

The drilling company asked me to stay with them. They had the opportunity to go to Brazil, India, or north. They'd been to India so that was out; Brazil was too hot so we went north. We went into Canada to Old Ontario to re-drill a gas seal on a natural gas well. When that job was completed,

Walt, the man I worked with on my tower, said, "I'm going to Great Slave Lake to build a rig; how'd you like to come?" I was eager to go. I was just a kid and he had taken me under his wing.

It took six weeks to get there because we took rig parts—heavy steel, timbers to build towers, and countless tools. We had two teams of horses, a cook, four drillers, and three builders. We went west to the Peace River, then 400 miles up the river on an old scow with a tug boat pulling us. From there, we went across country to the barrens to a narrow gauge railroad that took us across the tundra. The train pulled ten cars all filled with our supplies. The load was heavy. I stood on the back of the train and watched the weight of the cars push the wheels under water, then float up like a tide.

Our caravan passed a Mountie Police station on September 15. They told us we had to leave because we had no supplies for winter. We left the equipment. On the way home, we crossed the tundra on the same train we came in on. The train stopped and I went out to see why. That was the first time I'd seen caribou. A migration of thousands and thousands of them were going to lower land for the winter. There were waves and waves of them. They looked like a rolling ocean. We waited more than two hours for them to cross the track.

I never went back. Walt had a wife in Canada and stayed to work for gas companies. One of the men I worked with died a short while ago. He started the Keystone Drilling Co. and became quite wealthy.

*The Manistique Pioneer-Tribune* June 12, 1980

### A. Harold Bowman

Mr. A. Harold Bowman, 77, of Route 1, Manistique, died June 6, 1980 at 4:35 a.m. at Little Traverse Hospital in Petoskey, Mich.

He was born Nov. 2, 1902, in Mackinac County and spent the greater part of his life in the Gould City and Gulliver areas. He attended the Gould City Schools and was a life member of Lakeside Lodge #371 Free and Accepted Masons, a life member of the Escanaba Commandry #47RT, a member of the Ancient Accepted Scottish Rite Valley of Marquette, a member of the Ahmed Temple and also a member of the Chapter, and formerly served on the Schoolcraft County Road Commission.

He was employed for 40 years as president of Bowman Gas and Oil Co. of Gulliver until his retirement in 1966.

He married the former Jean M. Ogborne on December 19, 1952 in Marquette, Mich.

He is survived by his wife, Jean, of Manistique; one son, William H. Bowman, of Gulliver; one daughter, Mrs. Vaughn (Patricia) Bratten, of New Baltimore, Mich. and eight grandchildren.

Friends called at the Messier-Broullire Funeral Home beginning at 4:30 p.m. Monday, June 9, 1980.

Masonic Memorial services were held at the funeral home at 7 p.m. Complete funeral services were held on Tuesday, June 10, at the Messier-Broullire Funeral Home at 2 p.m. with the Rev. Max Weeks officiating.

Serving as pallbearers were: Vaughn Bratten, Isaac Pawley, William F. Bowman, Guy H. Bowman, Jay A. Bowman and Richard L. Ogborne.

William Phillion, York Anderson, Earl Jones, Ed Blanchard, Charles Rusiecki and J.L. LeDuc served as honorary pallbearers. Burial was in the Fairview Cemetery.

*Gould City Main Drag c. 1890 (Courtesy John Blanchard, Newton Township Historical Society)*

*Gould City, Unknown boy and girl*

86 ~ Huntspur and Along the Tracks

*Railroad photo Gould City, MI. The depot was moved from Corinne to Gould City in 1908. (Courtesy John Blanchard, Newton Township Historical Society)*

*Gould City Livery Stable c. 1900. L to R: Palmer Bowman, Bessie Bowman (Palmer's Daughter), Stanley Bowman in buggy, Earl Bowman in buggy, Deloss Baker with white whiskers, Almond Bowman, Hazel Bowman, Lyle Bowman (Courtesy John Blanchard, Newton Township Historical Society)*

*Logging Sled Group. c. 1908 Harvey May second from left, front row (Courtesy John Blanchard, Newton Township Historical Society)*

*Harry Salters Saw Mill near Gould City Railroad Depot c. 1920 (Courtesy John Blanchard, Newton Township Historical Society)*

## WILSON HOUSE MUSEUM
Newton Township Historical Society
Gould City, MI

(Courtesy Lucille Kenyon, Newton Township Historical Society)

The Wilson House was originally a store in Corinne, Michigan. After a section of Gould City burned down in 1930, the building was moved from Corinne to Gould City. Over the years, it has been a store, home, boarding house, barbershop, post office, and antique shop. It was purchased by the historical society in 2012. Museum hours have not been determined yet, but it will open in 2014.

## BERNICE ACKLEY

Mother cooked at a camp on Sandtown Road when one of my sisters got sick and she had to come home to take care of her. Father and I took her place. I was fifteen years old. A man driving a horse and cutter took us to camp. When we arrived, there wasn't a bit of cooked food in the place. I knew how to make bread for a family but not for ten men so I made biscuits. Father peeled vegetables, cut meat, and cooked them. We managed to feed the men until Mother arrived a few days later. Father left and I stayed the rest of the winter to help Mother.

My husband, Ted, and I courted in a horse and buggy and got married when I was eighteen and a half. My first born, Harland, was three years old and Olive was three months old when the cook at Mr. Frank Hartman's camp quit. I decided I wanted the job. The men didn't think I could do it with two babies. I told Mr. Hartman I'd like to try and he agreed to hire me.

I earned fifty dollars a month and got room and board for me, the children, and Ted. We had our own bed in the cook shanty. I was breast-feeding Olive and Harland was creeping and walking so I kept them in the kitchen to play while I worked.

My day began at five o'clock in the morning and ended about ten o'clock at night. The men came in from the bunkhouse before daylight so breakfast had to be ready before six o'clock. The men ate, Ted ate, then I ate, and the children ate whenever they got up. Ted helped me in the mornings, then left to cut short stuff in the woods. He came back before noon to help with lunch and stopped working in the afternoon earlier than the other men to help with the supper meal. The dinner bell rang exactly at six o'clock for breakfast, at noon sharp, and at five o'clock for supper. The men waited at the door until the bell rang, signaling they could come in to eat. The table was always set with hot food ready to be passed.

Cooking involved one thing right after the other. Breakfast was bacon and pancakes. When the men left, I cut up meat and peeled vegetables. I made something sweet every day from scratch—pies, cookies, or doughnuts. When the baking was done, I washed the dishes then set the table for lunch. I always tried to cook enough meat for dinner so there'd be enough left to warm up for supper. After lunch, I washed dishes and prepared for supper. After supper, I made bread to set and raise overnight, washed dishes, cleaned up the kitchen, and set the table for breakfast.

I was getting worn out. I got sick. I was pregnant and didn't realize it. Near the end of my pregnancy, I got so tired I'd sleep while the men ate lunch. Ted and a friend helped out. I had to quit in March. It was a hard job but I enjoyed it. I was healthy and am still healthy today.

*The Manistique Pioneer-Tribune* May 24, 1985

### Bernice M. Ackley

GERMFASK—Mrs. Ted (Bernice) M. Ackley, 86, Rt. 1, Box 29, Germfask, died Sunday, May 19, at 10:04 p.m. at the Schoolcraft Memorial Hospital.

She was born Aug. 15, 1898, in Bay City, Mich. She spent the greater part of her life in Germfask. The former Bernice Melissa Chase married Ted Ackley in St. Ignace on Nov. 21, 1916. She was a member of the Grace Lutheran Church of Germfask. Mr. Ackley preceded her in death Nov. 26, 1980.

She is survived by: four sons, Harland, Germfask, Lester, Germfask, Charles, Newberry, Theodore, Germfask; eight daughters, Mrs. Rinehart (Olive) Schroeder, Engadine, Mrs. Fred (Vivian) Losey, Flint, Mich., Mrs. John (Virginia) Dontrich, Tucson, Ariz., Mrs. Donald (Shirley) Sigl, Green Bay, Wis., Mrs. Charles (Betty) Niles, Fenton, Mich., Mrs. John (Janet) Rutherford, Seney, Mrs. Eugene (June) Brow, Newberry, Mrs. Henry (Delores) Ketola, Seney, Mich.; one brother, Harold Sandford, Clifford, Mich.; 49 grandchildren; 83 great-grandchildren; several great-great grandchildren.

She was preceded in death by two sisters, Mrs. Leonard Nettie Bebee, Mrs. George Mabel Vaughn.

Friends may call at the Messier-Broullire Funeral Home in Manistique beginning at 4 p.m. today. Funeral services will be held at the Grace Lutheran Church in Germfask at 2 p.m. on Wednesday. Burial will be in the Riverside Cemetery in Germfask, with Rev. Allen Park officiating. Visitation will be at the church prior to the funeral from 1 to 2 p.m. on Wednesday.

## FLORENCE HEMINGER
### March 8, 1980

I was born in 1907 in Marquette, Michigan.

I first worked at a camp in Eben Junction. It burned when I was twenty-two so I went to East Lake Camp toward the Soo, near Rudyard, to help my mother do laundry and to help in the kitchen. We washed sheets, pillow cases, shirts, and heavy wool underwear for one hundred men.

No matter how often we washed, we couldn't get rid of the lice and the bunkhouse had bed bugs. We washed the clothes in kerosene to kill the lice and sprayed the bunkhouse with turpentine to kill the bedbugs.

We washed two and three times a week in a big room with a wood-burning stove. We did all the washing by hand. We scrubbed the laundry on the scrubbing board, then boiled everything, but the wool in big tubs of kerosene water on the stove. We wrung the laundry out with a hand wringer, rinsed it again, and then wrung it out again. Wool can't be boiled or it'll shrink so we soaked the shirts and underwear overnight in kerosene. In the morning, we washed them in warm water, wrung them, and rinsed them. I hung laundry outside on a clothesline to dry. It was hard work. My fingers hurt from the cold. If the clothes didn't dry outside, we rehung them in the wash room. All the sheets and pillow cases were ironed with flat irons we heated on the stove.

The days we worked in the kitchen, we'd get up about five o'clock to start baking the bread and sweet rolls. We'd make the bread dough the night before, let it raise, then bake it in the morning. We made coffee, then set the table. There was always lots of food on the table—bacon, eggs, pancakes, and even hard tack. Canned peas, corn, tomatoes, and fruit came in by the carload.

We packed the men's lunches too. By the time we finished preparing for the next day's meal, doing dishes, and cleaning up, it was about nine o'clock at night. We did get to rest during the day. We couldn't have kept working without a rest.

I met my husband Chum at the East Lake Camp. We got married and moved to Huntspur in 1931 or 1932. We had good neighbors. Frank Heinz had a beautiful house near the railroad tracks. His brothers Bill and Lawrence worked for him. A.D. LaCroix was there. He had a big camp back in the woods. I knew him from his East Lake camp. Chum worked in the woods and I stayed home to raise our two boys, Lawrence and Ray. I had a nice garden and bought most of my groceries at the Heinz Store.

When the Huntspur lands were sold, we had to get out. We bought the house we are living in now from Frank Heinz and moved it to the Green School. This has been our home since then.

*The Manistique Pioneer-Tribune* September 6, 1984

### Florence Heminger

Gulliver resident Mrs. William (Florence) Heminger, 77, born March 22, 1907, died Wednesday, Aug. 29 at Marquette General Hospital.

She spent the greater part of her life in the Gulliver area, moving there in 1936 from Parkington, Mich. She attended Limestone and Marquette Public Schools.

The former Florence Marie Roy married William A. Heminger May 10, 1929 in Sault Ste. Marie, Mich. He died Dec. 10, 1977.

Survivors include one stepson, Herbert Heminger of Manistique, two sons, Lawrence and Raymond Heminger, both of Gulliver, one daughter, Mrs. Stanley (Dorothy) Kusmirek of Munising; one brother, Norman Ray of Marquette; two sisters, Mrs. Leo (Arbutus) Snyder of Gulliver, and Mrs. Lee (Pearl) Tweedale of Chatham; two step-grandchildren, nine grandchildren, one great-great grandchild, 21 great-grandchildren and one step-great-grandchild.

Friends called at the Messier-Broullire Funeral Home at 4 p.m. on Friday, Aug. 31. Services were held at the funeral home at 10 a.m. Saturday, with Fr. James Menapace officiating. Burial was in the Fairview Cemetery.

## VERNON (MICK) LEE

### FIRST SETTLERS IN CURTIS

My grandpa, John Lee, the first white man to live in Curtis, arrived about 1884. He lived with the Chippewa Indians in the hut of Chief Saw-Naw-Quato for eighteen months and was treated like family. After he moved out, they stayed friends.

In 1886 the Federal Government granted land patents to several Chippewa and one white man, my grandfather, John Lee. The property included the high bluff across from the present day Erickson Center and extended to the shores of South Manistique Lake. In recent years, the sand has been removed from the bluff and cabins and several houses are now on the shore of the lake. His house and barn were on top of the bluff exactly on the spot of the present day public parking lot.

My grandparents were the first white people to build a log house and a log barn in the area. It was in their house in 1888 that the first white person was born in Portage Township, my Aunt Rhoda. My dad, Neil, was born there in 1890. The first voter registration and the first election were held in that house.

I remember going to Grandpa's farm with Pa and my brothers in a horse and buggy. We played on a wooden gate held together with wooden pegs. To allow the gate to swing easily, a pole was attached to a spring and a pail of stones was attached to the pole.

One of Grandpa's fall chores was to cut dry cedar into fine sticks. During winter nights, the family sat around a wood stove as many families sit around a television today. Grandpa would light one of the cedar sticks and hold it in his hand for their light source.

Pa said he and Grandpa fished every day from a canoe they kept on the shore at the bottom of the bluff. They fished along the north shore and caught all the fish for the day's meals in a very short time. They ate boiled fish every day. People didn't fry fish as we do today.

Grandpa was a farmer and a drayman. A drayman is a trader. In those days, people didn't have money; they bartered. He'd leave home in the morning with his horse and buggy and perhaps a chicken, milk, eggs, or potatoes. He would go from house to house trading. Pa said he'd leave in the morning with a few things from the farm and come home with a wagon full of items.

One winter, Grandpa and a teamster (a man who drove a team of horses) hauled supplies for a lumber company with a horse and sleigh. The supplies were carried in a wooden box four feet high, eight feet wide, and sixteen feet long. The box had several trap doors on the top. To keep the wolves away, lighted lanterns were hooked onto the sleigh and chains were dragged behind because they made noise, which didn't always work.

One night, they were hauling freshly butchered meat from Newberry to Camp A. A pack of snarling wolves tried to attack them. The teamster drove the horses and Grandpa climbed onto the wooden box, opened a trap door, and threw out several pieces of meat for the wolves to eat so they could continue on safely. Pa said Grandpa was really scared.

I didn't know my grandma, Mary Lee. She died in 1895 when Pa was five years old. What I do remember is that family members said she was a small, strong woman. Before a well was dug near their house, she carried two buckets of water at a time from the lake back up the bluff to their farm. The buckets hung from a carved wooded yoke she carried on her shoulders.

After Grandma's death, Grandpa married a widow, Margaret Anderson. Between them, I believe there were twenty-one children. Times were tough. There wasn't enough food to feed everyone. Unfortunately, we don't know a lot about those days. Pa didn't talk about it much. But things happened that would never happen today.

Aunt Rhoda and several of her sisters were told to bundle the few clothes they owned into a piece of cloth. They were put into a horse drawn wagon and left at the end of various farmers' driveways hoping the girls would earn their room and board. Rhoda and her sisters ended up in the orphanage in Marquette.

Dave Hern, a teacher who lived on the SW corner of the intersection of H33 and Sandtown Road, brought Pa to his house to live. Mr. Hearn's original house is still there. Whenever we visited Curtis, Pa always stopped there and let us drink from a flowing well in the yard.

Pa began working in lumber camps at an early age. He was working in Bryan for Stack Lumber Company when he met William Moe. William invited Pa to dinner and that's where he met his future wife, Gertude Moe, my ma.

The night they got married, they stayed in a company shack in Bryan next to the railroad tracks. Family, friends, and neighbors had a chivaree. They stood outside their house and pounded on pots and pans, sang loud, hollered, pounded on the buzz saw, and made loud noise.

*Main Street Bryan, Michigan*

### MY EARLY YEARS

I was born in that run-down company shack on August 21, 1918, the third of five boys. My real name is Vernon, but everyone knows me as Mick. We were dirt poor. Highway US 2 wasn't much better than a horse and buggy trail and the first ten years of my life I never traveled more than nine miles from home.

We were living in Bryan and I was about six years old when US 2 was being built. There were no tractors or trucks. Gravel was dug out with horses and slush scrapers; then men hand-loaded it with shovels into two feet by six feet dump boxes on wagons. The horses pulled the wagons to the middle of the road where the gravel was dumped; then a crew spread and leveled it with shovels. After they dumped the load, my brother Bob and I jumped into the empty wagon and rode it back to the gravel pit.

Stack Lumber closed logging operations at Bryan in 1923. We moved from Bryan into a log house next to Grandma and Grandpa Moe. The company kept the store and Bryan School in operation that winter, and Pa drove us to school with a horse and buggy. There were only nine students in the whole school. Mrs. Elva Gilroy was our teacher. She completed the eighth grade and the school board hired her to teach us.

## THE DOC

Bob hurt the bottom of his foot when he was about seven years old. He limped around most of the summer; then it became so painful he couldn't walk. He was in terrible shape. Aunt Rhoda visited one day and said, "You get that boy to a doctor."

Uncle Archie hooked up the horse and buggy to take him to Doc Toms and I went with them.

Doc Toms lived on the hill along US 2 where Michihistorian is today. The Doc farmed, cut a little timber, and did a little doctoring. He had no office, no hospital, no medication for pain, and Penicillin hadn't been discovered. If you got hurt, he just worked on you.

We went into his living room and he looked at Bob's foot. He said it was a stone bruise that had to be lanced. He told Bob to crawl head first on his belly under a couch. Bob scooted in until just his legs were sticking out. Doc told him not to move; then he told Uncle Archie to hold his other leg so he couldn't kick. Doc bent Bob's knee up and with a quick flick of the wrist, lanced the foot. Bob couldn't get out and couldn't move. He was stuck under the couch. Did he holler!

## THE BIG TRIP

Uncle Charlie lived in Traverse City. He gave Grandpa a pacing horse. Uncle Archie went to Traverse City and walked the horse home, about one hundred and sixty miles, and he had to cross on the Mackinac Ferry with it. I can't remember how many days it took.

That horse was our transportation for many years. Grandpa made a seat and a wooden box four feet wide and six feet long to sit on a wagon frame and he adjusted a harness to fit the horse. The first time Grandma went to Gould City to buy groceries, she took us boys with her. The night before, she warmed flat irons in the oven. In the morning, she harnessed the horses and wrapped the irons in rags to keep them warm. We sat on the seat bundled up with our feet on the irons. Grandma drove, the horses trotted along, and a couple of hours later, we were in Gould City. She hitched the horses to the hitching post outside May Healey's store, gave the horses hay, and covered them with a horse blanket. May fed us a lunch; then she and Grandma visited while Junior, Bob, and I played outside. We helped Grandma load the groceries into the wagon box; then she trotted the horse home. That was an exciting day.

## GOING TO SCHOOL IN GOULD CITY

Pa drove us to the Gould City School with a team of horses and a homemade school bus: a small house that fit on the wagon box. In winter, he transferred the house onto runners. He put two little glass windows in the front to run the reins through. If it was warm, he'd leave the windows open. He sat on a box looking out the front, and we sat on benches along the side with split firewood stored underneath for the small wood stove near the back door. As we traveled along, he'd stop and pick up kids.

Several teams of horses with homemade houses like ours brought kids to school. Rusty Bellville drove a team from the east; Ed Leveille drove from the south. Ed had a beautiful black and gray. I can still see the horses pulling up to the school, letting the kids off, then pulling away. The school board supplied feed and boarding during the day at the Gould City livery stable.

We didn't go to school in the spring and fall because the road flooded and the horses couldn't get through. When we went in the winter, we might stay only three or four hours because of the seven mile one-way trip. If a bad storm came up, we'd have to leave.

US 2 was completed in 1929 and plowed regularly. Pa bought a '29 Ford truck, put the homemade house on the bed, and earned sixty dollars a month to drive kids to school. Now we could go to school in the fall and spring and winter. The kids from south of Gould City continued coming with horse and sleigh on rolled roads for several years because plows didn't keep the side roads open.

## SNOWBOUND

The fall of '29, Pa drove us to school in the '29 Ford truck, and then the winter turned savage. We were snowbound for six weeks. We didn't see a soul outside of our family. The wind blew the snow and cold between the cracks of our log house. We woke up in the morning with snow on our blankets. My brothers, me, and Fanny, our dog, slept together in one bed. Fanny crawled under the blankets and slept on our feet and kept them warm.

We moved into a shack in the field. It was just a frame house with boards nailed to the studs and tar paper on the outside, but it was warmer than the log house. We ran out of flour and sugar so Grandpa and Pa walked to Healey's store in Gould City. A snowplow had gone through earlier in the year and made a bank that froze hard enough for them to walk on. They returned home, each carrying a sack on their back. One carried fifty pounds of flour and the other carried fifty pounds of sugar.

We spent our days fishing inside our fish house on Pike Lake. We'd get ten to fourteen pike a day. Uncle Archie walked to Blaney every day on the packed snow trail to work in the woods. He came home one night and told us a rotary snowplow was at the Blaney Corner coming along US 2 from Manistique. The whole family sat at the window watching for the plow. We never went to bed, none of us. We stayed up all night. Early in the morning, we could see the reflections of the plow lights coming from the county line. At daylight we could see it.

It was a big Ford Wheel Drive truck; FWDs they called them. It had a V plow with a shaft and fan rotaries on each side throwing snow. It broke down in front of Grandpa's house. A man drove an old pickup truck behind the plow, carrying a supply of gas for the plow. The road crew left in the truck, and we went out and played on ten-foot-high snow banks.

The crew came back about a week later and got the plow going. They continued on and met a plow coming from the east. In a few days, the first car we'd seen since fall came through—a Model T.

**SELF-SUFFICIENT**

We never went without food, not even during The Depression. We had three or four cows, a hen house full of chickens, a sow pig, and a team of horses. We fished and snared rabbits. Every year, the sow had two litters. We fattened the pigs on sugar beets and started butchering the piglets in summer when they dressed sixty to seventy pounds. We ate one a week. As the pigs got bigger, it took fewer to fill us up. We had a big garden, a root cellar, and basement shelves stacked with canned venison and vegetables from our garden. We plowed three acres just for potatoes. Bob, Junior, and I picked wild berries every day when they were ripe. Grandpa made a wooden rack and attached straps to it like a pack sack for Junior to carry because he was the biggest. Bob and I carried three two-quart pails. We didn't go home until they were filled. We walked to Bryan, two and a half miles, to pick raspberries and blackberries. We picked blueberries in Fergey's Marsh and strawberries close to home in the clearings toward Pike Lake. Sometime in the 1930s, Rector built a resort at the lake. They threw empty jam jars into a dump and we'd wash them and use them.

In the spring, we tapped Maple trees and boiled sap to make sugar candy and syrup. Grandpa Welch and Grandpa Moe made a shack for us to stay in. We always planned ahead. We hauled hay in for the horses in the winter when the ground was still frozen. We had to cross two swamps to get to the sugar bush. When we got to the swamp Kenny, Junior, Bob, and I climbed onto the horse and rode it bareback through the water. We carried our groceries in washtubs. We hooked a chain through the washtub handles then attached the chain to the dray stakes. The washtub floated through the deep water and kept our food dry.

During the warm months we killed deer, cleaned them, and cooked them, all in one day. We put the cooked meat into crocks and poured deer fat over it. The fat sealed the meat and kept it from spoiling for up to a month. When we wanted meat, we took some out of the crock, warmed it up, and then poured the fat back into the crock. That was our refrigerator.

Every fall, Grandma said, "You boys pick two bushels of apples and kill two deer. It's time to make mincemeat." Junior and I were the hunters in the family.

In late November or December, before the deer yarded up, we'd shoot five or six deer at once. We cleaned them, cut off their feet, and hung them from a branch in the woods. We didn't have a rope so we put a stick through their head and hung them between two branches. In the winter, we'd put on our snowshoes and bring them home as we needed them. We seldom ate beef; we needed the cows for milk.

My youngest brother, Donny, was born in 1929. Ma had a stroke shortly after he was born. She stayed in the hospital in Manistique for two and a half years. Her right side was paralyzed. Grandma and Grandpa lived across the road and helped some but Pa and we boys took care of ourselves. We all helped raise Donny and continued our daily work as before. After a few weeks, a work pattern emerged. Kenny, the oldest at fourteen, became Donny's main caretaker. Junior did the cooking and inside work, and Bob and I did the hunting and outside work. We survived.

### WAYFARING STRANGERS

During the deep part of The Depression, 1931 or 32, it was not uncommon to see men walking along the highway or a husband and wife carrying children, looking for a place to stay, sometimes begging for food. One day a man came walking up the driveway. He was so weak he had to lean against the wood shed. He said, "If you could feed me, I'll be glad to do some work for you."

Bob and I went into Grandma's house and told her a man was outside asking for food. She invited him in. Bob and I stood by the door and watched. On the table were homemade bread and butter. She told him to sit down, but he just grabbed a piece of bread and shoved it into his mouth. She put a bowl of stew on the table. He grabbed another piece of bread and dunked it into the stew; he didn't even ladle it into the bowl. He ate standing up. He ate and ate and ate. He was starving to death.

He said to Grandma, "Now I ain't got no money, but I'll cut some wood if you'd want."

She said, "No, we got lots of wood. You don't have to do nothing. We don't need help."

He thanked us.

Bob and I followed him out the door. He walked a short distance, laid down in the ditch, and fell asleep. I've often wondered what happened to him.

In those days, we trusted strangers. People were honest in spite of the hard times, but we did have something stolen. A man came to our door and asked if he could borrow our tea kettle to fill the car radiator with water. He walked to his car, got in, and drove away with our tea kettle. We weren't sure if we should have gotten mad or if we should have laughed, but we certainly were dumbfounded.

## KELL'S CAMP

The winter of 1932, I stayed at John Kell's camp and drove a team of horses. I still laugh when I remember the pigs in the manure pile. Kell kept pigs to slaughter. They weren't penned; we fed them and they stayed close to camp. I was walking to the barn one morning after a heavy snow and the manure pile came alive; it looked like it was rolling. Horse manure holds heat and the pigs slept in it for warmth. The snow covered them like a blanket, and when they heard me, they roused out.

I worked at Kell's until spring break-up, and then went back when the ground thawed and dried to drive a team of horses that jerked railroad ties out. The steel rails had been removed from the Bryan Grade but the ties were left. We'd leave camp just at daylight and return to camp before noon with a load of ties. We walked twelve miles before lunch and the same thing after lunch. I drove the team twenty-four miles a day.

After the ties were out, we graded the road. Ed Thayer drove the team on the grader, John Kell, the boss, rode the grader, and I drove the tow team on the grader. We graded the road from Bryan to Camp Twelve. We opened that road.

I worked so hard during the day that my legs automatically kicked during the night. The older man I slept with cut a snorting pole and put it under our mattress. The pole made a hump so I couldn't roll to his side of the bed. I wore holes in the bottom of my work boots walking through the sand. I cut cardboard and put it over the soles, but the sand kept getting into the shoes and my feet started to bleed. I went home one Saturday and Pa had a new pair of boots for me. I turned fourteen that summer. I got a dollar a day and my board.

### HAYING AT BLANEY

The summer I turned sixteen, Junior and I cut hay on a farm near Blaney where Harold Peters, a game warden, lived. We hitched a team of horses to a hay wagon and brought our crock of freshly cooked venison (shot out of season), potatoes, and some milk in a jar. We cut the hay with scythes and stacked it with pitchforks. The first two nights, we tied the horses and slept under the wagon on the ground. Harold Peters came on the third day and said, "Boys, this isn't a very good place for you."

I said, "We don't mind it here."

He said, "You come and stay in my garage and put the horses in the barn."

We slept on the garage floor covered with a blanket. Harold gave us a kerosene stove burner and offered us meat, but we didn't need any but our milk had spoiled. Harold had a gentle Jersey cow. One morning, Junior dumped potato peelings outside the garage window and the cow came to eat them. I went out and milked her. I filled a small can. Harold would have told us to take all the milk we needed, but we were bashful and wouldn't tell him our problems.

## WE DIDN'T WORK FOR MONEY; WE WORKED TO SURVIVE

No human being should have lived the way we did the winter of 1935. It was terrible. Ernie Derwin hired Junior and me and four others to work on a logging job one half mile off the North Bryan Grade Road. We skidded cedar trees that had burned and blown over to make a thirty by twelve-foot shack. The trees were dry and light and easy to handle. We cut balsam poles for the rafters and put a twelve-foot partition in the back for Aunt Ethyl and Uncle Charlie. They cooked for us that winter. We hauled in double bunk beds and a wood cook stove from Kell's abandoned camp. We dug a hole in the dirt floor to use as a root cellar and covered it with a trap door. We put up a barn for the horses.

Our only light was a two quart canning jar filled with grease. We cut up old underwear for a wick. We slept in the double bunk beds next to the burned logs and our clothes turned black and smelled like smoke. We dug a hole in the swamp and it filled with water. The horses drank out of it and that was our dipping water. We'd drop the bucket in for the horses to drink, and when they were done, we dropped the bucket again for us to drink. Ethyl made bread every day and we ate meat and potatoes. That was it.

Toward spring, the cutters finished their work and left so we didn't need Ethyl and Charlie. John Ehn, Junior, and I stayed. John and Junior skidded logs to the landing and I cooked, took care of the horses, and shoveled snow.

One Saturday, I walked six miles home to get supplies. Junior and John were supposed to stay and work. Sunday afternoon, Pa drove me as far as the Bryan Grade Road; then I walked to camp carrying a gunny sack filled with thirty pounds of oats, two loaves of bread, and some butter rolled up in a cloth. When I got to the shack, Junior and John weren't there and I could see they hadn't skidded any logs.

I stayed alone Sunday night and Monday night and all day Tuesday. I was so lonesome. At night, the howling coyotes made me feel lonelier.

I used my time. I peeled cedar railroad ties inside the shack. I opened the trap door and put a peeling horse next to it. I'd carry a tie in, peel it, and kick the bark into the hole, then carry it back out. That's what I did for two days: peel ties. On Tuesday, I decided to go home. I set out water for the horses and fed them lots of hay. I walked out of the barn and saw Junior and John returning to camp. They had walked to Curtis and got drunk. They were still buzzed up when they got back.

We made thirty-five dollars that winter and gave it all to a neighbor for a milking cow we needed.

## OPEN HOUSE

The upstairs of our house was one big room with beds lining the walls. People were always welcome—relatives, friends, and strangers.

My older brothers, Kenny and Junior, were walking along the street in Gould City during hunting season where they met two hunters from southern Michigan who were looking for a guide. They didn't know the area and hadn't seen a deer. The hunters said they were renting a cabin near Curtis. Junior told them we were hunters and could guarantee them a buck. He said, "Get your bags and stay at our house."

They were at our house within an hour with all their belongings. They slept upstairs and ate at our table. They stayed until the end of deer season. That was how we met Mike Kenny and Rocky Lockwood.

The following year, they rented a cabin at Rector's Resort to be near us. A few years later, Mike bought a large piece of property on Pike Lake not far away. We built a log cabin for him. Mike and his crew liked being around us. We became lifelong friends.

## SMOKEY RUBY

Smokey Ruby was our friend. His name was Edward but we always called Smokey. Mrs. Ruby died when Smokey was young and he and his dad continued living in their shack at Ruby Bay. One evening, Smokey arrived at our door to tell us his dad was dead. Junior, Bob, and I walked with him back to the bay. We laid his dad out on the table. Junior washed the body and covered it with a blanket. The afternoon of the funeral, Pa said, "Boys, you'd better get Smokey; he needs a place to live."

I can still see him walking along the trail to our house with everything he owned in a white pillow case slung over his shoulder. He moved in with us. He lived with us until he was drafted, and when the war was over, he got off the Greyhound Bus at our driveway. He was like a brother. He was part of our family.

## SMOKEY GOT SHOT

One hot summer day, we walked to the lake to swim. We always carried a gun. We'd break it apart and each carry a half. I put the stock under my shirt and Smokey put the barrel under his belt and down his pant leg. On the way home, we walked along an old moonshine trail toward Bryan where we had seen a big bear. We wanted to shoot it. Smokey took the gun and walked to Kell's abandoned dynamite shack. Kenny, Junior, Bob, and I were to chase the bear to him. We made a lot of noise. We got to the shack and Smokey wasn't there. Then we heard him hollering, "Help, help." We could see his head bobbing up and down above the grass and we thought the bear had him.

He hollered again, "I'm shot! I'm shot!"

He hadn't removed the gun barrel from his pant leg when he put the stock on and the gun was loaded. He shot the top of his foot. He leaned on us as he hobbled to the road. A car came into sight and we ran into the road to stop it, but it drove onto the shoulder and kept going. I realize now what happened. We were pretty rough-looking and waving a gun and they probably thought we'd shoot them. Donny was young, twelve or thirteen, and he heard the commotion and drove to us.

We took Smokey to the Shaw Hospital in Manistique. Doc Shaw said, "I'll have to report this. When the police get here, tell them you were target shooting." And that's what we did.

The hollow point Super X bullet went inside Smokey's boot and traveled down both sides of his foot. The doctor said it'd do more damage to take the bullet out than to leave it in. He didn't want to cut any muscles. It never bothered Smokey, and years later when he died, the bullet was still in his foot.

We often shot deer out of season. The game wardens knew but couldn't catch us so when Ernie Derwin, the game warden, heard about Smokey's accident, he said, "Don't worry about them. They'll all shoot themselves." I heard about that comment. Ernie liked to drink. That winter he was driving drunk and ran into a snowplow. I said, "Don't worry about those drunks; they'll all kill themselves."

## THE KAVOS

Smokey had three half-brothers whose last names were Kavo: Inor, Tony, and Willie. Inor died at the age of twenty-five working in the woods for Heinz Lumber Company in the Green School area. A branch fell on him. Bob, Junior, Kenny, and I were pallbearers.

The Kavos made whiskey, drank a lot, and fought amongst themselves.

They lived on H 33 near Burton's gravel pit. One Saturday night, several Kentuckians living in the backwoods drove a Model T Ford to Kavos' to drink and party. Tony and the Kentuckians got into a fight and Tony bit the ear off one of them. The Kentuckians left to come back with reinforcements. They told Tony they were coming back to cut off both of his ears and they threatened to kill him. It was late at night when Tony knocked on our door to tell us the Kentuckians were coming back to even the score. At daybreak, we all walked along US 2 and found the Kentuckians' empty car stuck in the ditch by Doc Toms. We figured they were so drunk they drove the car off the road and walked home. We found two knives on the front seat. The Kentuckians never carried through on their threat. The last time I saw Tony, he was in Gould City. He opened his trunk and inside was a little box. Inside the box were a dried ear and two knives. He carried them around like a trophy.

### ARGUMENT

A tall, lanky man, a drifter from Kentucky, worked at Rector's resort the summer of 1939 for his room and board and a small wage. Several times, we walked to his cabin to visit, but we never got real friendly and I don't remember his name. One night he said, "Could you guys shoot me a deer for a guest from Ohio?"

Smokey asked, "How much is in it for us?"

He said, "Five dollars for the hind quarters."

I said, "We'll be back tomorrow night with it."

We shot a little buck, dressed it, and put the hind quarters in a white cotton sack. The following night, we returned to his cabin, knocked on his door, and said, "Here's your meat."

He said, "Okay, you wait here and I'll bring the money back." He came back, put five dollars on the table, and said, "I get half that."

I reached over and grabbed the money and said, "No, you don't. You told us you'd give us five dollars for a hind quarter of venison and that's what you got."

He said, "I should get half for selling it."

Smokey said, "You should have collected more money; this is our money." So we got into an argument.

We started to leave and he said, "I'd shoot you guys for that."

And I said, "By God, you'd better make a good shot because if you don't, you'll never make another one."

## SHOT IN THE BACK

I was shot in the back on the third day of hunting season about one-thirty in the afternoon the 17th day of November, 1939.

Smokey and I were driving deer in the swamp for Mike Kenny, Rocky Lockwood, and their crew. I saw a big deer in a slashing and I thought it was a buck. I shot and crippled it. It was really bleeding. It ran thrashing through the woods. Smokey came over and I said, "Goddamn, I shot a doe."

Smokey said, "It went past me too. I thought it was a buck, but I couldn't get a clear shot."

It was getting close to noon so we picked up the hunting crew and ate lunch at our house. It'd give the wounded deer a chance to settle down.

Smokey, Don Seagull, and me walked back to get the deer. We saw human footprints in the heavy frost that weren't there when we came out for lunch. I said, "Someone's here." We were uneasy about the footprints but continued on, cautious.

We tracked the doe into the slashing and back onto an old logging road and that's where we jumped it while it was lying in the tall grass and that's where I got shot. The road curved like a half moon. The deer got between Smokey and me. Smokey was on one end of the curve and Don and I were at the other end. The deer got up and I aimed to shoot and that's when I was hit in the back. I never fired my gun. Don heard shots, saw I was hit, and hollered, "Smokey shot Mick." But Smokey didn't shoot me. He was in front of me and I was shot in the back. Smokey was headed south and I was headed north.

Don went crazy. He ran through the woods toward the cabins on Ruby Bay where Mike parked his car. He was hollering, "Smokey shot Mick! Help; come right away!"

I never went down, not even when I got hit. I should have lain down; I was gushing blood. I walked almost a half mile out, leaning on Smokey. By the time we got to the road, I was so weak I was staggering. My lungs were filling up. Smokey said, "I'll kneel down and you sit on my knee." I put my arm around his neck to hang on.

One car passed on the highway and I said, "Smokey, get into the road and stop the next car that goes by." I was getting weaker; I knew I'd had 'er.

Then Smokey said, "Here comes a car," and I looked up and Mike Kenny's car was barreling down that old grade to beat the hell. Mike drove and I sat in the middle. I sat up all the way to Manistique. Mike drove the car wide open. I don't know how we made it.

Doc Shaw was raking leaves in front of the hospital. He dropped his rake and ran toward us and Mary Steven and Adel Cooper, two nurses, held the door open. I was getting weaker, could hardly stand up, but I walked in with help from Mike and Smokey. They cut my shirt off and the bullet fell out on the floor. The bullet went in my back, hit my bones, and mushroomed out my left arm.

Mike said, "What do you think, Doc?"

Doc said, "He's hit hard. He's lost a lot of blood."

Mike said, "I'll take care of the bill."

They took x-rays. Then Doc Shaw said, "I'm going to give you a shot and put you to bed."

I said, "I want to walk," and started for the door and that was the last thing I remember for four and a half days. I started to rouse out in the night. A little dark nurse from Garden was sitting beside my bed. "Vernon, is there something you want?"

I could hardly talk. I wanted water and she gave me a drink, but I barely had the strength to swallow. That afternoon I ate a little. I was in the hospital for twenty-one days.

Junior was working as an apprentice undertaker in Manistique and he came every morning and night to see me.

When you live through something like that, it's luck. They didn't give transfusions and they didn't have Penicillin. The doctor didn't do anything to me. They cleaned me up, fed me, and watched for gangrene.

I came home from the hospital just before Christmas, and it was in March before two state police came to our house to fill out a report.

The cops said, "You must have turned. You had to be looking the other way."

I said, "No, I wasn't looking the other way."

They filled out a police report stating Smokey's bullet went past me, ricocheted off two trees and then hit me in the back. I had to sign the report saying Smokey shot me and I'd press no charges. That was the killer of the whole thing, signing that paper.

The report, the conclusions the police came to, were stupid, but we didn't want to tell them what the trouble was. They never knew the whole story. As a matter of fact, nobody ever knew much about it. We kept it pretty still. Smokey, my brothers, and I were the only people who knew what happened. No one else in the family knew and this is the first time I've told about it.

The Kentuckian was never seen again after I got shot. Bert Rector said he figured he left on the Greyhound Bus that night. He left because he knew he'd get killed. He knew he was treading on shallow water for what he did that fall of '39 on the third day of deer season.

In the spring, when it dried up, Smokey and I went back to where it happened. He asked, "Where were you standing?"

I said, "Right here." We walked along the trail a ways and came to a small Balsam.

Smokey said, "Mick, look here. Here's where my bullet went. I couldn't have shot you." His bullet hit a small Balsam and went through it. It traveled from the north and blew woodchips out the south side. He had shot at the deer and missed it.

We never discussed it; we never told anyone; we kept our mouths shut. We didn't want the law investigating.

*The Manistique Pioneer-Tribune* July 2, 2009

### Vernon "Micky" Lee

(August 21, 1918 - June 27, 2009)

Vernon "Micky" Lee, 90, of 3577N Lang Road, Gulliver, Michigan died June 27, 2009 at Marquette General Hospital in Marquette.

He was born August 21, 1918 in Bryon (Newton Township), Michigan, the son of Neil and Gertrude (Moe) Lee.

He attended the Blaney Park Elementary School and the Gould City School.

On December 28, 1940 he married the former Dorothy M. Hastings in Manistique.

Micky was self-employed and enjoyed the work and challenge of the day. Over the years, he was a cattle and horse buyer, a timber buyer, a builder, a woodsworker, a lumberman, and also bought and sold real estate. He also worked as a bus driver for the Mueller and Manistique area schools for a number of years.

Micky was a great story teller, always enjoying a good laugh and the company of others. He also enjoyed trout fishing and hunting, when he could.

He is survived by his wife, Dorothy M. Lee of Gulliver; daughters, Lois (David) LaRose of Manistique; Jane (John) Kopecky of Gulliver, and Sally (Don) Hughson of Gulliver; eight grandchildren; 15 great-grandchildren; four great-great grandchildren; along with nieces and nephews.

In addition to his parents, he was preceded in death by an infant son in 1942; and his brothers, Arnold "Junior" Lee, Quentin "Bob" Lee, Kenneth Lee and Don Lee.

Visitation will be held from 11:00-1:30 pm, Tuesday, June 30, 2009 at the Messier-Broullire Funeral Home in Manistique. Funeral services will follow at 1:30 pm, at the funeral home with Reverend Jay Martin officiating. Burial will follow in the Fairview Cemetery at Manistique.

Memorial donations may be directed to the Bay Cliff Health Camp.

## EDWARD (SMOKEY) RUBY OBITUARY

*Republican News & St. Ignace Enterprise*

St. Ignace, MI - 49781, Thursday, July 14, 1966

## MILITARY RITES ACCORDED - VICTIM OF HEART ATTACK

Military rites will be accorded this morning at the graveside of Edward (Smokey) Martin Ruby, 47, victim of a heart attack which caused his death at two o'clock Sunday morning.

Mr. Ruby, a veteran of World War II, resided on Rte. 2, St. Ignace. He lived most of his life in western Mackinac County and for a time at Gulliver. At the time of his death he was a woodsman working with William Gamble.

Born in Newton Township on Sept. 30, 1918, he was the son of the late Mr. and Mrs. Martin Ruby.

Surviving are a sister, Mrs. Eva Young of Flint, a half-sister, Mrs. Sinja Light of the Soo, a half-brother, Anthony Kavo of the Soo, and a number of nieces and nephews.

Funeral services will be conducted from the Davis funeral home at ten o'clock this Thursday morning. Burial will be in the Gros Cap cemetery.

Pallbearers are to be Leonard Michelin, Eldred Becker, Frank Rickley, William Gamble, George McCall and William Boahbedason.

Officiating at the rights will be the Very Rev. H. Vaughan Nortor.

*The Hunting Crew c.1930, standing on left, Bob Lee, boy sitting in front, Kayo Moe, Mick Lee far right, others unknown. (Courtesy of Dean Lockwood collection)*

*Bear Hunting c. 1940, left kneeling, Junior Lee, right kneeling, Rocky Lockwood; back left, Mick Lee, back right, Mike Kenny. (Courtesy of Dean Lockwood collection)*

*Kell Camp. c. 1930. Logging camp located near Curtis on H33. L to R: Eric Morrison, Cecil Morrison, Laura Kell McLean, Alex Creighton, Mildred Kell Spomer, Lilly Nelson Farley, Mae Johnson Hutt, Violet Kell Creighton, three unknown, two unknown children, unknown worker, Faunie Kell, Jonathan Kell. (Description and photo courtesy of Sally Setterlind)*

## KENNY LEE

*William and Bessy Moe residence, October 5, 1947 going from left to right Junior, Mick (in front) Smokey (back) Bob (front arms crossed) Kenny (behind) Gertrude (mother) Neil (father) Donny*

I was fifteen years old when I began working full time with Pa and my younger brother, Junior, at John Kell's Lumber Camp. Pa drove a team of horses skidding logs and Junior and I skidded pulp. It wasn't far from home so we walked to work.

We worked in snow that came up to our crotch and wore bibbed overalls to keep the pitch off our wool pants. The overalls got wet and froze stiffer than a poker. One day Junior was acting smart and cut his bibbed pants off to the depth of the snow. Old Kell came along, shook his head, and said, "He's crazy."

I was going on eighteen when I stayed in camp steady. If a camp didn't feed the men good, they couldn't keep a crew. But that winter was tough times, the Great Depression, no money. The Gould City School even shut down for a while. Kell's camp was the worst camp for feeding men, but no one quit. Jobs were hard to get. The pancakes were so sour we covered them with peanut butter and syrup.

Lights went out at nine o'clock, no talking or someone would throw a shoe at you. When men got up in the middle of the night to take a leak they'd piss out the back door. It was solid ice back there, too slippery to walk on.

We dried our mitts and socks on a pole next to the big wood stove in the middle of the bunkhouse. We slept in our wool underwear on wide bunk beds, two men on the bottom bunk, two men on the top bunk with two wool blankets, no sheets. Heat rose from the wood stove and the top bunks got hotter than hell. I was a teamster so I slept on the bottom bunk because I had to get up an hour earlier than the other men to feed, water, clean, and harness the horses before breakfast. Matt Mann woke early to start the fire and wake everyone up. He'd grab your big toe, then the next guy's. Nobody slept in.

After I took care of the horses, I sat by the kitchen door and waited for the six o'clock breakfast bell. I was the first one in. It was pass this, pass that. No talking. We got fed three times a day. Sunday we got fed but it was a light lunch.

I drove the same team all winter. They were my responsibility seven days a week. Besides getting up early to take care of them, I brushed, fed, and watered them as soon as we came in from the woods. I also oiled and checked the harnesses to make sure they were in good working condition.

I had been working a few seasons for Kell and he was paying me pretty good money, but I quit. Our house was a few miles away from camp so one Sunday I left lots of feed for the horses and walked home. When I got back, Kell said, "If you don't stay here on Sunday to take care of the horses I won't pay you as much." Monday morning I fed and watered the horses and left the harness on the wall. I told Kell I was done.

Tony Kavo and I went to work in the Finn Camp on H 15, just before Brotherton Road, down in the swamp. Tony's family and mine knew each other for years. Tony's dad died in 1912. He got pinched between two train couplings. Grandpa Moe told me that he and another man took him to Pike Lake on the pede but he died a short time later.

Tony and I were the only men in camp that spoke full English; they spoke Finnish and Polish. We logged all summer with horses and a heavy wagon. The bunkhouse had a hole in the floor with boards laying over it. We washed our hands over the boards and dumped the dirty water down the hole. It got to stinking pretty bad. That was the only time I got lice.

It was prohibition and everyone in the area made moonshine but Grandpa Moe and us. Tony and his mother made moonshine, and one night, Tony got drunk and got into a fight with a Finn. Tony bit the tip of the Finn's ear off. The Finn left and was driving back in a Model A with some of his friends to cut off Tony's ear. They were so drunk they wrecked the car before they got to him.

The fall of 1933, Frank Heinz came to our house to ask me to drive horses at his camp in Parkington. Uncle Moe was driving a team and they got away from him so Frank told him not to come back. Men were fussy about who handled the horses. You can't be mean to them, no hollering, and you have to know how to hold the lines, and what they can and can't do.

I worked for Frank all winter, six days a week, and two Sundays I loaded logs onto train cars. I made two cents more an hour than the other men because I was driving a team. I came home that spring with sixty dollars. Inor Kavo said, "Boy, I wish I had a stash like that." It was the height of The Depression.

Leo and Bill Heinz, Frank's brothers, worked with us at the Parkington camp. Leo was a blacksmith and the strongest man I ever met. We wrestled and I couldn't hold him down so Inor and I both took him on. The two of us couldn't lick him.

I stayed with Heinz Lumber Company for a few years, and in 1935, went to work for Webster Lumber Company north of Newberry. That was the year the government signed the NLRA (National Labor Relations Act) and we got an eight-hour work day. But we didn't get paid for walking. Sometimes the job would be five miles from camp. Older men might ride the dray. A man forty-five or fifty years old was considered old so I'd put boards across the dray for them to stand on. There were no seats. I hung my lunch pail on the harness and walked beside the dray, holding the reins.

The snow was deep and like sugar. A cedar saw is four feet high and it got buried in the snow. When I drove my teams off the ice road to haul the logs out, the horses were in snow up to their collars. I hooked small logs on first and worked back to break a trail through the snow. I walked steady from the time we left camp until twelve noon when both the men and the horses got a one hour break.

While the swampers (men who cut the trees and brush to enable the horses and drays to get through) built a fire, I took the horses' bridles off and fed them six quarts of oats. We packed our own lunch. I didn't like cooking frozen bread over the fire because it burned on one side and the middle stayed frozen, so every day I packed thirteen boiled eggs, gingersnaps, and hardtack. I'd lay the eggs beside the fire to warm and the men would laugh, "You going to set a hen?"

Toward the end of afternoon, if I gauged the horses were up to it, I used them to break a trail for the next day's job. It'd give the ground a chance to freeze overnight.

No one had to tell us to go to bed at eight o'clock.

A guy we called Ugly Guss stayed at this camp. He'd get ugly, go to town Saturday night to get drunk, and come back Sunday night. He didn't like anybody sitting on the bench in front of his bunk. I sat on his bench one day and he said, "You go to the end of the camp to sit," and I said, "You go to hell." But I still gave him a ride on the dray.

The next year, Webster Lumber Company asked Earl Robare and me to work for them in Wabashaw, Minnesota. We drove horses, then worked in the mill making railroad ties. We earned thirty-five cents an hour. Webster cut back on our hours so we took a job in northern Minnesota where we felled trees to make dams for flood control on the Mississippi River. From there, we went to Brownville, Minnesota where we cut logs with a cross-cut saw. The first day on the job there were twelve gangs of men; twenty-four men, one man on each end of the cross-saw. At the end of ten days, there were only six gangs working. I said to Earl, "I don't think we'll last long here." But they kept us until the season ended in March. We were small, which was to our advantage. We weren't allowed to cut trees higher than two feet from the ground. Sometimes we had to cut only eight inches above the ground. Just imagine how hard it'd be if you were a tall man bending over to saw eight hours a day? You couldn't do it.

We were expected to clear-cut one acre a day but our foreman said we were only cutting three-quarters of an acre a day.[3] He stood on a stump with a measuring pole and watched us. We didn't stand around and we didn't rest.

---

3      Clear cutting one acre of timber with a cross-cut saw was an Olympian-type feat. It required extreme skill, endurance, and strength. Very few men, even from this age of extreme physical work, could accomplish this task.

The foreman was a little man, smaller than me. He was a drunk and on Monday mornings when he showed up, his eyes looked like two piss holes in the snow. He'd pull his coat up around his head and the tobacco juice ran down the side of his mouth and dribbled onto his coat. He reminded me of a rat.

On this job we made sixty-six cents an hour. We were in big money. I sent eighty dollars home for Christmas. My room and board was one dollar a day, and in the evenings, Robare and I each drank one beer that cost ten cents.

I came home in March and worked for Webster again at a mill in Corinne sawing railroad ties. I lived in the back room of a bar and boarding house with the mill crew. About 1940, I worked construction when US 2 was being upgraded. I leveled cement for sixty cents an hour. Those were long days. After that, I tended bar for Ernie Blanchard until I got drafted.

I worked in logging camps about ten years. The camps were home to a lot of men. That's all they knew. They had a place to live, food on the table, and all they had to do was work.

*Heinz Parkington Camp*

*2nd from left 1st row, Leo Snyder, Earl Robare, unknown, Kenny Lee (with open shirt and dog's head at his feet. On right are 3 men Frank Heinz is on the end in the middle wearing black shirt and pants.*

*The Manistique Pioneer-Tribune* August 27, 1981
## Kenneth Lee

Kenneth M. Lee, 66, Rte. 1, Box 175, Gulliver, died Saturday, Aug. 22 at his residence.

He was born Oct. 26, 1914, in Gould City and spent his entire life in Gulliver and the Gould City area. He came to Gulliver on March, 1947 from Gould City.

He attended Gould City Public Schools. He served in the U.S. Army during World War II. He was employed as a shovel operator at Inland Lime and Stone from March 4, 1946, to March 1, 1975. He was a member of the Inland 25-Year Club.

He married Alicia M. Hastings in Columbia, S.C., on Oct. 21, 1944.

He is survived by his wife, Alicia; four sons, William and James, both of Gulliver, Ronald of Belleville, Mich., and Thomas of Newberry; two daughters, Mrs. Robert (Judy) Berry of Rapid River and Mrs. Robert (Jenny) Henkel of Roseville, Mich.; two brothers, Vernon and Quinton of Gulliver; and 11 grandchildren.

Funeral services were held on August 24 at 2 p.m. with Rev. Keith Swartz officiating. Burial is in Newton Township Cemetery.

## WESS EMERY

## THE BEAVER SCANDAL OF 1931

One night there were thirty-two beaver trappers in the Newberry County Jail and I was amongst 'em.

I was cutting pulpwood that winter for a lumber company for ¾ cents a stick; seventy-five cents a day, so I trapped a little on the side. At that time, the price we got for our beaver hides would more than pay for your fine.

The Conservation Department had what we call today a sting operation. They knew there was lots of beaver trapping going on and they were trying to catch the buyers and trappers. They sent a man up here to pose as an illegal fur buyer.

I sold that man twenty-two blankets of beaver for twenty dollars apiece. That was four hundred and forty dollars. That was a lot of money.

I started trapping that fall in November and trapped through till January when I got caught. The law asked me what I had done with four hundred and forty dollars. They wanted it back. I had a family and I was poor so I told them I wasn't giving the money back. It was mine. I had earned it. The judge sentenced me to twenty days in jail and the sheriff let me go on the nineteenth day. They never did get the money.

Most of the other trappers arrested gave the money back and were sentenced from three days in jail to a ten dollar fine.

The Conservation Department held a six-week grand jury investigation. Trappers and suspected buyers were questioned but no one was arrested. Nothing ever came of it, none of the trappers would squeal. A lot of the furs were going into Canada. The Conservation Department requested the Canadian government's assistance with the investigation, but, of course, it was not in the Canadian Government's best interest to get involved. Trapping was legal there.

Buyers from the Soo, Phil Jacobson, Smaller, and Brody, smuggled the furs across the border. From there they went to New York, and many went on to the European markets. The other main market that I know of went through Chicago.

Word got around, "Here's where you can get rid of the beaver." One of the buyers I sold to was Isackson. He owned a junkyard in Manistique. The price for used steel and iron was fair and people came and went throughout the day, buying or selling. In addition to the local steel market, he also shipped carloads of iron by rail to Chicago. Furs were smuggled with the rail shipments.

It was a typical junkyard. There were several old shacks and sheds scattered among piles and piles of iron, steel, and old motors.

The office didn't look much better than the old shacks. I don't think it was ever cleaned. When you entered, you'd see an old desk to your left, and to your right, a wood stove, several chairs, and a spittoon. Shelves cluttered with junk lined half of the back wall. An oil and dust film covered everything except the paperwork on the desk, which moved at a pretty rapid pace, but even those were covered with oily finger marks. In spite of the dirt, a fair amount of light came through a window near the desk.

On the back wall where the shelves ended was a door to the back office. This is where the fur trading was done, usually at night or on a Sunday, but sometimes during the regular weekday. If it weren't for the layers of dirt, you'd think this back room was a ritzy banker's office. A big heavy oak desk sat in the middle of the room. Two black leather chairs faced the desk. Under the desk and chairs was an expensive rug. When we came in with our furs, he'd pull the curtain over the window, then we'd slide the desk and chairs off the rug, roll the rug back, and lift up a trap door. He stored the furs in hundred-gallon wooden barrels right under his desk. People were in and out of that front office all day and never suspected the hides were there.

It was common knowledge that he bought illegal furs, but only a few of his men and us trappers knew where he kept them. He was summoned to a Grand Jury Investigation by the Conservation Department, but he was never caught.

Another fur buyer was Pete Olson. He had a little country store at the Green School. Pete was short and didn't weigh much. He had a white mustache and lots of white hair that he kept clipped to ear level. He wore the same clothes day after day; a plaid flannel shirt and dark green Soo Wool pants. He had a habit of wiping his nose by running his finger under it. His shirtsleeve was hard and crusted from dried snot. I doubt if he took a bath more than once a year. He didn't wash his hands and the undersides of his fingernails were black with dirt.

The store wasn't any cleaner than Pete. One day, we had furs lying on the counter while we were discussing a price when a woman came in to buy some meat. When she opened the door, Pete slid the furs into the meat freezer next to the counter. The woman ordered some meat. Pete wiped his nose with his forefinger and placed the meat on the same counter the raw furs had been.

Another time, a kid asked for an ice cream cone. Pete wiped his nose, reached into the freezer, and scooped the ice cream out of a bucket. The lid to the ice cream was damaged and didn't fit properly so he placed a fur over the top. The next time I went to sell Pete furs, another kid came in and asked for ice cream. Pete lifted that dirty fur from the top of the can, scooped the ice cream, and replaced the fur on top of the can. By then, the fur had frozen to make a handy cover.

Pete had a clever way of hiding his furs. His garage roof was flat and slanted slightly toward the back so the water would run off. It had a false front about four feet high, but it also had a false back and false sides about two feet high. Standing on the ground, you could only see the false front.

He'd pay me for the furs and then walk out onto the back step and fling those furs up over his head onto the garage roof. No one could see them. That's where he threw his fresh furs, and that's where he dried them, and that's how he eventually got caught. Time passed and the DNR got planes. A DNR plane was flying over and saw those little round things on the roof. He bought furs for years and years before he got caught and for years after he got caught.

***

Well, the day after they let me out of jail I grabbed my packsack and was back in the woods again.

Tucker, a lifetime friend and fellow trapper, and I went in on the West Branch of the Two Hearted River to an old log cabin. The cabin was about ten by twelve feet. It wasn't big but the logs were big pine, probably fourteen inches in diameter. People called it Old Tom's Cabin. I don't know what this feller's last name was, but they found him dead in there one spring. He was an old trapper.

We stayed in Tom's cabin. It was in bad shape. The only place it didn't leak was just over the place we slept.

After we set all our traps, we walked onto a big beaver dam. There was a path over the dam created by the beaver. On both sides of the dam, the water was shallow for a long ways out. We started walking into the shallow water. You could hardly wade in there even with hip boots, it was so mucky. A dry tamarack was sticking up in that mud. It looked like it had been a stake. I took hold of that stake and was working it around to get it loose.

Tucker said, "What are you going to do with that?"

"I'm going to get it loose; I'll use it to set a trap."

"Where are you going to set a trap?"

"It's a good stake; I'll save it for when we need it."

I pulled it out and there was a No Four Newhouse trap, our standard beaver trap.

Tucker looked at me and said, "You old bastard, did you know that was down there?"

"No, I didn't, but I did want that stake."

We set the trap right there, and the next morning, we had a big beaver. When I got done skinning him, I held his nose up even with mine. He was so big that all of his tail and some of his bottom were lying on the ground.

\*\*\*

Trapping was an awful job and hard work. We had to carry those raw beaver skins a long way. We walked. The snow had just melted and we walked the whole way in hip boots. We each had two packs full of green beaver hides. Each pack weighed between eighty and one hundred pounds. We walked to what we called the Iron Camp back north of McMillan then into Camp One; both were old logging camps. We walked from Camp One and crossed the Two Hearted River at Hemlock Dam. Then we went in on another lake and a creek we called the Wart. From there we hit the West Bank and the North Bank [of the Two Hearted River].

From the day we left Old Tom's Cabin, we had nothing but trouble. It rained the whole week. We had a pup tent with us. The bread got wet so

I'd fry the bacon and then I'd fry the bread to kill the taste. The bread got so damned sour we couldn't even fry it anymore. We threw it out at Camp One.

I carried a piece of fishing line in my pocket. We'd either dig those little white worms from just under the bark of dead pine trees or cut a little slice of bacon and use it for fish bait. We ate fish day after day. Fish don't ever look good to me anymore.

After we left the North Branch, we struck right out across country and came out on the road near McMillan. We never arranged for anyone to pick us up because we never knew when we'd come out, so we walked the twenty miles home during the night. In those days, we walked for miles and days and nobody ever worried about us. We never used a compass. I never even learned how to read a compass 'til I was pretty near thirty years old.

We sold those furs to Jacobson in the Soo. He had old buggy wheels he'd cut the spokes out of. He sewed the skins in them buggy wheels to dry. He didn't use boards. He didn't have a buggy wheel big enough to sew that big beaver I had trapped. We sold it to him just as it was.

I had a hell of a bankroll. I bought a brand new 1929 Ford Sports Roadster. It cost me $665.00.

***

One winter, I snow-shoed into Tahquamenon country and camped ten days alone in my pup tent at the Eagle's Nest. It was quiet and lonely. There wasn't a chickadee, or blue jay, or nothing around. Not a sound.

I got up early the first morning and set traps. The second morning, I checked my traps. I had a beaver. I carried it back to my campsite. I sat right down and skinned it out and left the carcass for the birds. After that the blue jays, and the chickadees, and the lumberjacks followed me around so I was always hunting things for them to eat.

## *The Manistique Pioneer-Tribune* June 12, 1980
## Wesley A. Emery

Wesley A. Emery, 74, of Gould City, died June 4, 1980, at Bell Memorial Hospital in Ishpeming. He was born July 2, 1905, in Moddersville, Mich. and spent the greater part of his life in Gould City and McMillan.

He attended the Houghton Lake Area Schools and was a member of the Rock River Lodge #524 Oddfellows at Gould City and was also Past Grand of Lodge #524.

Mr. Emery was employed as a woodsman.

He married the former Nora Wheeler in Manistique on October 23, 1973. He is survived by his wife, Nora, of Gould City; one son, Jerry Emery, of Vermillion, Ohio; one step-son, Raymond McCarrick, of Houghton Lake; two brothers; William Emery of Higgins Lake and Frank Emery of Cadillac, Mich.; three sisters, Mrs. Gordon (Bertha) Norman and Mrs. Erin (Ruth) Vanburg both of Merret, Mich. and Mrs. Lloyd (Helen) Keilholtz of Alma, Mich. and three grandchildren.

Friends called at the Messier-Broullire Funeral Home beginning at 5 p.m. on Friday, June 6. Complete funeral services were held at the funeral home on Saturday, June 7, at 2 p.m. with Rev. Austin Patty officiating.

Burial was at the Woodlawn Cemetery at Curtis, Mich.

# JUDGE QUINLAN
## Told by Wes Emery
### THE JUDGE WENT VIOLATIN'

Late one night, Pike and the probate judge from Newberry, Judge Quinlan, were out shining deer in the McMillan area. Pike was driving and the judge had the gun. Pike stopped the car and the judge shined the light into Red Atkerson's pasture and saw two eyes. The judge took careful aim and shot. Down went the deer. The men jumped over the fence and ran to the deer to gut it.

There lay Red's dead horse. Both men were upset. A good man never admitted he mistook a horse for a deer, and worse, Red would probably call the police in the morning and an investigation might be held. Even if he didn't report it to the authorities, word would get around quickly and several people knew the judge and Pike were out violatin' that night.

Pike and the judge went back to the car, quietly drove down the road a ways, and waited a few minutes to see if any lights came on in Red's house. Nobody stirred.

The judge had a plan. Knowing Red was not an early riser; he and Pike would go to Red's early in the next morning and wake him. They wanted to talk with him before he had a chance to go out into his pasture and find the dead horse.

The dew was still heavy when the judge and Pike knocked on Red's door. The judge knocked several times more, louder. Finally, Red answered the door. They had gotten him out of bed.

Red said, "What's wrong?"

The judge said, "Nothing's wrong, Red. I came here to buy your horse."

Red said, "He's not for sale."

The judge said, "Red, I really like your horse; name your price."

Red's desire for money was stronger than his desire for the horse so he agreed to sell it for a goodly sum.

The judge said, "You drive a hard bargain, but I do like that horse so I'll pay you. Now, while you're getting dressed, I'll write you out a Bill of Sale."

When Red returned, he signed the Bill of Sale and the judge paid him the money.

Red, Pike, and the judge walked out to the pasture. The horse wasn't waiting at the gate as he usually did, so Red whistled. The horse didn't come. They walked through the first pasture and into the field. Red whistled and the horse still didn't come. He grew concerned. They walked a short ways into the field and Red saw the horse lying on the ground. They all ran over to it. Red knelt down and saw the bullet hole between the eyes.

Red looked at the horse in disbelief and then looked at Tucker and the judge. "What the hell...?" Realization showed on his face. "You shot my horse!"

The judge said to Red, "No, that isn't your horse; that's my horse, and I've got the papers to prove it. Now, I have a problem. I have a dead horse in your field and I have to bury him. I'll pay you a good sum to do it."

Red said, "Sure, but it will be a good sum."

The judge told Pike that the price of that dead horse was high, but it could have been terribly higher.

To my knowledge, that was the last time the judge went violatin'.

### NOTE FROM THE AUTHOR

At one time, a majority of people considered poaching a right, a way to survive, and a way of life. During the Great Depression, it became more like a battle between the Sheriff of Nottingham and Robin Hood, and game wardens were the enemy. Poaching laws were little more than small hurdles to jump over as the runner continued around the track. Locals didn't use the term "poaching"; they called it "violating" or "violatin'."

Anyone who used the word "poaching" was suspected of being connected with law officials. A stranger who said "poaching" was never to be trusted. He was "closed out."

*Newberry News* September 24, 1954

### John E. Quinlan

John E. Quinlan, supervisor of McMillan Township, and former Judge of Probate of Luce County, died Sunday morning at the Tahquamenon General Hospital, after an illness of the past several weeks. He was 79 years of age.

Judge Quinlan was born in Fayette on March 29, 1876, later moving with his parents to Manistique. He was married to Elizabeth Deemer in Manistique on Sept. 20, 1898, and the following year moved to Garnet where he was in charge of the store operated by the Manistique Iron Co. In 1905 he came to Newberry to take charge of the iron company's store north of Newberry and in 1906 was placed in charge of the store and the company logging operations.

In 1907 he acquired ownership of the Murphy Hotel in Newberry from the firm of Murphy & Gormely and conducted the business with success until 1918, when he disposed of it to Lyle McLean.

He was elected Judge of Probate in 1920, which office he held with distinction for 28 successive years, retiring from office in 1948. He was a past president of the Michigan Association of Probate Judges. In 1949 he was elected supervisor of McMillan township, which office he held at the time of his passing.

Besides his wife, Elizabeth, he is survived by four children, Mrs. Merle Teeple of the Sault; Clifford of Detroit; John of Newberry; and Mrs. Elizabeth Taylor of Newberry; two sisters, Mrs. N.J. Detzler of Newberry, and Mrs. Floyd Duell of Chehalis, Wash; three brothers, Peter, David and Lawrence, all of Newberry; nine grandchildren and four great-grandchildren.

Funeral services were held in St. Gregory's church Wednesday morning at nine o'clock, with Rev. Emil Beyer celebrant and Rev. Jos. Callari and Rev. Ralph Sterbenz, subdeacons. Interment was in Forest Home cemetery.

## MURDER IN SENEY

Prior to the murder of Patricia Burdick it was common for people to trust strangers and hitchhike without fear. Her murder was so shocking and disturbing it changed that innocent and trusting way of life.

*Escanaba Daily Press,* Thursday April 26, 1956

### Parolee Admits Slaying Grand Marais Teacher

### Body Is Found Hidden In Brush North of Seney

Manistique—A Marquette State Prison parolee, 35, was to be arraigned here this afternoon for the first degree murder of a pretty 21-year-old Grand Marais school teacher whom he has admitted bludgeoning to death with a wrench. Leonard Lundberg, of Munising confessed to state police today that he had killed Patricia Burdick to still her cries after he tried to seduce her in his auto off lonely M77 between Grand Marais and Seney Sunday night.

Early today the bachelor parolee had pointed out to police the spot in a desolate pine forest five miles north of Seney and a mile west of M77 where the teacher's body lay covered with pine branches and straw.

### UNDER FALLEN PINE

The body was found under a fallen pine tree near the east branch of the Fox River, just over a light hill off a side trail. It was fully clothed in the red coat and khaki slacks she was wearing when she disappeared, except one shoe was missing.

The parolee led detectives to the swampy spot where he said he dumped the girl's body. Shivering in the freezing midnight rain, Lundberg refused to look at the corpse.

The spot was part of an area which had been covered only Wednesday by a search party which had been looking for the girl since her mother, Mrs. Eva Burdick, of Sault Ste. Marie, had reported her missing three days ago.

### WAITED AT JUNCTION

Miss Burdick was last seen Sunday night at the intersection of M28 and M77 in Seney, where she was waiting for a ride to Grand Marais. The ride would have been the last leg on her customary weekend hitch-hiking trip to see her mother in the Sault.

A Marquette man had dropped her off at the intersection and continued on to Marquette.

The accused killer told State Police Det. Sgt. Anthony Spratto that he was en route Sunday night from Munising to his uncle's cabin on M77 between Seney and Grand Marais. He said he stopped at the Seney crossroads and offered the girl a ride as far as his uncle's place.

After driving several miles north, he said he parked on the shoulder and made advances toward the girl. When she began to scream, he said he grabbed a car wrench from the floor and beat her in the head with it.

Lundberg said he then turned around and drove back to within five miles of Seney, turned off on a side road and drove a mile into the woods, where he dumped the body.

### CALLED OFFICER

The trail which led police to Lundberg began when the alleged murdered called Parole Officer John Elmquist and asked to see him. Elmquist told state police. Then Upper Peninsula State Police headquarters in Marquette learned that Lundberg had not gone to his job as a timekeeper at the Munising Wood Products Co., in Munising.

Spratto and Zeni spotted Lundberg's 1949 sedan parked on a side street in Marquette Wednesday morning. They found the right side of the front seat spattered with blood.

Lundberg, who was in Marquette to ask his parole officer for permission to go to Detroit, spotted the detectives examining his car. He went to the Marquette city police station and turned himself in.

### CROWD JEERS

When police escorted Lundberg from Schoolcraft County Prosecuting

Attorney William Sheahan's office today a jeering crowd of about 20 persons gathered on the street, shouted, "Kill him; lynch him!" There was no violence.[4]

## CAN'T TELL

### By an Anonymous Interviewee

Do you remember when the teacher from Grand Marais was murdered?

It was late April. We were violating. It was dark. Tom and I set two hundred foot gill nets in a small lake north of Seney off M77 and then left.

When we came back later to pull the nets, we met only one car on M77 but we had to be careful. We didn't want to take a chance on anyone seeing us turning toward the lake. About a half mile before the turn-off, Tom stopped our pick-up and disconnected the taillights. He turned off the headlights. We turned into the lake road and drove really slow, watching.

We saw a car backed up to the lake. The interior lights were on and a man was standing at the shore of the lake scooping water into his hands like he was washing them; then he stood and threw some water from his cupped hands into the car. He was so busy he didn't notice us.

Tom said, "What the hell's going on?" He backed the pick-up to the main road and parked it in an abandoned driveway. Ten, maybe fifteen minutes later, the car came out. We scrunched down in the seat. We looked over the dashboard. One man was inside.

We waited until we felt safe, then went to the lake and pulled the nets.

We hadn't heard about the murder yet.

Later, we figured the man we saw that night was the man who had murdered the teacher and that he was washing the blood off his hands and trying to clean his car. We didn't dare tell anyone because they'd ask, "What were you guys doing there?"

---

4   The police removed Richard Lundberg from the Manistique jail to Marquette earlier than planned because a larger mob was forming than reported in the newspaper. Groups of men were planning to charge the jail and lynch him.

## PART THREE: THE CICERO CONNECTION

Cicero, Illinois is in Cook County, the same county as Chicago, but it is not part of Chicago. Al Capone moved his criminal organization to Cicero from Chicago because the Cicero police were friendlier. Cicero government officials, past and present, have a reputation for political scandal and connections with criminal persons and organizations.

## JOE KOPECKY
## 1990 Interview
## March 1911-October 1994

We heard lumbering camps in Minnesota were hiring lumberjacks. It was 1930 and my brother John, our friend, Frank, and myself, decided to go there to work. We were broke with no transportation so my girlfriend, Blanche, offered to finance a car for me. We found a beautiful used open Ford Roadster in good shape for one hundred and sixty-five dollars. It had chrome, a rumble seat, and the windshield came down. Blanche gave me one hundred and fifty dollars and I added the fifteen dollars.

My friend Lester had recently married and moved to the outskirts of a little town in Northern Minnesota. He always wanted to be a farmer so he rented an eighty acre farm near his wife's family. He asked me to bring a bed and mattress from his mother's house in Oak Park.

We strapped the mattress and bed frame on top of the car and put a dresser in the rumble seat and covered them with a canvass. We carried thirty-five gallons of gas in five gallon cans. Gas was eleven cents a gallon, but if you bought over ten gallons, it cost only ten cents. We saved a penny a gallon.

We left Cicero in late November, and before we got to Wisconsin, it started snowing. It really came down. We drove all the way, 633 miles, in a blizzard. The side curtains were full of holes and the wind and snow blew in. The only warm spot was near a manifold heater on the floor opposite the driver's side. It got hot by your feet, hot enough to burn your shoes, but the heat didn't get to the rest of the car so we took turns driving and sitting by the heater.

We continued through Wisconsin and arrived in Minneapolis early in the morning. Frank was driving. He began to fall asleep at the wheel. Our car headed toward a group of people waiting for a streetcar. John grabbed the steering wheel, alerting Frank of the danger. We almost ran into the crowd. Frank pulled to the side of the street and John got in the driver's seat. We sat for a few seconds, waiting for our heartbeats to slow.

As we got further into northern Minnesota, the snow began piling up in the road and the wind got stronger. Visibility was poor. We were worried about being stranded in a blizzard. We knew we were near our destination and continued on. We passed several farms. I heard somebody holler, "Joe!"

We stopped. Lester came running toward us, a silhouette in the snow. "I recognized your Roadster. I was worried. I've been waiting at the end of the driveway."

He lived in an old farmhouse with no electricity. He had one lamp in the kitchen and candles in the other rooms. It was twenty-seven degrees below zero outside and cold inside.

We helped him assemble the bed and put it into his bedroom.

Lester told us the lumber camps shut down because they didn't have orders for logs. There was no work. We were disappointed.

We unpacked the food we brought, and his wife, who was pregnant, warmed it up.

We had a good visit and went to bed early.

Frank, John, and I slept in one bed. It was cold. The wind came through the cracks in the wall and through the cracks in the window frame. The curtains were blowing. We took turns sleeping in the middle. We slept in our clothes and heavy overcoats. We got up in the middle of the night and took a bearskin rug off the floor and found some old carpets and used them for blankets. When we got up in the morning, the drinking water in the bucket was frozen solid. We started a fire in the kitchen stove and warmed up frozen stew we had packed. Lester's sweet wife was not much of a cook and they didn't have extra food.

We got acquainted with the neighbors. Word got around we were from Chicago and people were overjoyed to see somebody from the outside to talk with. They invited us into their homes for meals and they always expected John to play the concertina. I guess you could say, we sang for our supper. They were good people; they laughed, in spite of the fact that many of them were losing their farms. It was hard times.

Lester's brother-in-law, Harold, asked us to cut firewood. His wife was a former schoolteacher and they had two little kids. One evening, after work, he invited us to stay for supper. His wife said to Frank and me, "Would you go into the cellar and get some potatoes?" She gave us a big milk pail and we filled it to the hilt. When we came up, she looked at the pail and smiled because she figured we had a lot more than we needed. But she cooked them all. She made mashed potatoes and cooked deer liver.

Frank never liked potatoes, but when that big pot of potatoes was passed around, he kept filling up his plate and filling up his plate. I kicked him under the table and he handed the bowl to me. She looked at me; she knew what I did. She said, "That's all right, I'll get some more; there's a lot more; don't worry about it." So Frank and John, who didn't like potatoes, ate potatoes. When you're starving, everything's good.

After supper, John played the concertina and we visited. They asked us about Cicero and if it was true that people got shot with machine guns. I said, "Once in awhile," but it wasn't like it happened a lot.

I didn't want to tell them about all the crime there.

I did tell them about the time John and I were young, playing in the prairie, (a block or two of treeless grass) when a boy came running down the street hollering, "Capone's dead! Capone's dead! Someone shot Capone." We ran to a barbershop a few blocks away and on the sidewalk lay a dead man, riddled with bullet shots. Someone thought they were killing Capone, but they shot a flunky who swept floors.

We left Harold's about one o'clock in the morning to go back to Lester's. My Ford wouldn't start. The oil was too heavy for the weather. The lights went out in the house and we didn't want to disturb them so we went into the barn.

It smelled of cattle and manure and was full of cats. We lay down in the hay near a big pile of rutabagas. The kittens played and climbed on our heads most of the night, but it was warm and we slept well.

The next morning, Harold came into the barn and found us sleeping. When we told him what had happened, he was upset that we hadn't knocked on his door. We got the car going; then he invited us in for breakfast before we headed back to Lester's.

Lester's farm was about ninety miles west of Duluth, near the mouth of the Mississippi River. It was wild, undeveloped country. He needed food and he asked us to help him kill two deer he had seen in the woods near the back field. John had hunted before so Lester gave him the gun and told him to stay by a boulder next to a deer run. He took Frank and me deeper into the woods. We were to make a lot of noise. The object was to spook the deer into running along the deer path toward John.

We hollered and clapped our hands and made all kinds of noise but didn't hear a shot. When we got to John, he said, "I never saw a deer."

Lester couldn't understand that.

### SHOOT HIM AND KILL HIM

I told a neighbor, Dave, I'd like to shoot a deer for Lester. The following evening, Dave knocked on the door and said, "I shot a little doe. It's about one mile from here, dressed out and hanging in a tree. I'll need your help to carry it out; bring your car. When we get it to my place, we'll put it in your trunk."

It was about eight o'clock and the moon was up when we arrived at his farm. His two small children were asleep. Dave said, "I'm acquainted with the game warden and sometimes he stops to visit. If he comes while we're gone, my wife will pull the shade down on this window facing the river. If the shade is up, all is clear."

John carried a rifle and Frank and I had our pistols. We walked about a half mile on the river. It was as narrow as a street, frozen, and looked like a white ribbon. Then we left the river and walked another half mile into the woods to the tree where the deer was hanging. It didn't weigh more than a hundred pounds and we took turns carrying it on our shoulders.

When we neared the house, the shade was up, but Dave said, "I don't trust the game warden and I want to play it safe. He sometimes parks his truck beside the highway behind some bushes near the bridge and you can't see it. I'll go ahead and whistle if it's clear."

He walked ahead a few steps, then turned back and said, "If the game warden comes upon you, shoot him and kill him, or you'll go to jail and they'll take your car!"

Frank and I took out our revolvers and John readied his rifle. We were prepared to kill him. About five minutes later, we heard a whistle. I put my revolver in my belt, picked up the deer, and began carrying it toward the house. Frank kept his revolver out and John kept the rifle racked. All was safe. We put the deer into the trunk and closed it.

We went inside and Dave brought out some homemade beet wine. He kept filling our big cups. John brought in his concertina and we sang Bohemian songs and some English songs. It was about one o'clock in the morning before we left.

Many times I've mentioned this story and my friends say, "Joe, you would never shoot anybody; you'd never kill anybody."

But you must remember those were different times. If I lost the car I had nothing. I believe we would have killed him to save our own hides. We would have done it. Otherwise, we would never have thought of killing anybody outside of war.

We were in Minnesota about ten days when we received a letter from Blanche telling us Dad was sick and we should come home.

We left on a clear day. Lester's wife made us sandwiches of deer meat and pork. She said, "If you should get stopped by the law along the highway, they won't be able to tell this is deer meat. The pork will mask the smell and taste."

As we were bidding goodbye, John said, "I have to confess; the day you took us hunting, both of those deer went past me. I saw them, but I got 'buck fever.' I couldn't shoot."

Lester said, "I knew something wasn't right; I was positive those deer would run past you."

## INCIDENT ON THE HIGHWAY

We were heading south when we passed a game division truck going north. They turned around and came after us with the siren blowing. We pulled the car to the side of the road and two officers approached. We got out and they asked, "Have you got any deer meat?"

We told them, "No."

"We'll have to look inside your trunk." I opened it. John had broken apart his rifle for traveling and the officer said, "What's this? What's the rifle for?"

John explained it was a gift from a friend. He took out a paper written by Harold to prove he owned the gun.

"Okay, okay. Why are you here?"

John told him we came looking for work but didn't find any.

The officer said, "Well, we have to watch you foreigners."

I turned to him and said, "I resent that; we're not foreigners; we're Americans."

He said, "Well, don't get yourself excited. We call all outsiders who come from other states foreigners."

"You shouldn't use that term."

He changed the subject. "Do you have a cigarette?"

I didn't smoke, but Frank and John did, so they gave each man a cigarette. They talked with John and me while they smoked and Frank stepped back to smoke alone.

The officer spotted my loose chains in the trunk. He reached in and took them out. He said, "What about this?" He thought we had traps.

"Those are skid chains for the tires."

"Oh, okay, okay." He handed them to me. I put them back and closed the truck. They told us they had stopped a butcher from Minneapolis with a truckload of Christmas trees. Under the trees they found fifteen deer he bought from farmers for five dollars apiece. They confiscated his truck and everything in it and arrested him.

They saw our sandwiches, but they didn't pay any attention to them.

The officers finished smoking, bid us farewell, and headed back north.

We continued on south, and after a few miles, John said, "Well, we're safe."

Frank said, "We were always safe," and he pulled out his loaded pistol from inside his coat.

## BACK IN CICERO

We arrived home just before Christmas, happy to see Dad had recovered from his sickness.

Blanche and I became officially engaged to be married. We returned from a date about three o'clock in the morning. She lived four doors away so I walked through the alley to my house. I had to pass a big truck parked in front of a garage. Men were unloading slot machines into a garage. Guys with loaded machine guns stood guard. They saw me and pointed their guns at me.

"Who's there?"

"Joe Kopecky."

"Oh, it's just Joe. He's okay."

I talked for a few minutes then walked on home. I didn't like what they were doing. I lived there, I knew them, but I never got involved with them. I never took money from them. They were hoods.

Between 1931 and 1933, I couldn't get work anywhere. I'd stand in line to apply for a job and two hundred people would be applying for the same job. In 1934, John and I got a job at the same time. The Bohemian Lodge hired me to dig graves at The Bohemian National Cemetery, and John got a job making mattresses. Sometimes I'd bring home six or seven dollars a week. It was a good job for the times. I worked several years at the cemetery, then got a job at the county hospital. I quit after six months. I didn't like it. It was misery on misery. Blanche and I were married and Patsy was a baby. I was afraid I'd bring sickness home. My boss said, "Don't leave until we find a Cicero man to replace you. Otherwise, a Chicago man will get the job and we'll never get it back." I stayed until they hired a replacement.

A friend had a beer route and I worked with him several years before I got hired by the Chicago Fire Department. I was very fortunate.

## CHICAGO FIRE DEPARTMENT

Our station got a one alarm fire call at a known gangster building in Chicago. As we arrived, three men were running into the building. The fire chief ordered them to stay out, but they ran inside, and a few minutes later came out carrying ledger books. When the fire was extinguished, I walked into a second floor room. A safe was open. Inside was thousands of dollars. They took the books and left the money.

*1930 Frank left, John Kopecky playing concertina (Courtesy Kopecky Family)*

*1930 John Kopecky left, On the road (Courtesy Kopecky Family)*

## BLANCHE KOPECKY

### August 3, 1912-January 1995

Emmy and Jim Swaney lived several doors away on South 57th Court in Cicero. Jim was a car dealer. Later, we learned he got into trouble with some mobsters. Emmy asked Dad to drive Jim to the railroad station. The next day a roadster with four men in it kept driving around the block. We could see the guns. They circled the block and circled the block. We were so scared. They were looking for Jim. Emmy called a few days later to say she had to leave. We don't know where they went and they never came back.

Stan and Julie, Emmy and Jim's son and daughter-in-law, moved into the house.

Julie was a secretary to the president of Cicero and met Stanley Swaney at a town meeting. She married him not knowing he was a mobster.

Stanley was head of the slot machines for Capone. The Ship was a big gambling joint across the street from Western Electric. Western Electric employed thousands of people so The Ship had a profitable gambling location.

Whenever the law was going to raid the joint, Stan got advance notice. What do you do with the slot machines? Move them out in a hurry. They moved them two doors down from us into Stanley's garage. He never kept cars in them; he used them to store slot machines. And Stanley's basement was full of slot machines. The raids were usually on a Sunday morning as that time interfered with the least business. Newspaper stories reported the FBI was breaking slot machines and shutting down gambling, but they weren't. The good machines were in the garage and basement. The old broken ones were left in the joint to get smashed.

Stanley called Dad one night and asked if he could store some slot machines in our garage. Of course, Dad couldn't say, "No." When they arrived, his men took the money out of the machines and put it in a little shed next to the garage. I was little. I was wearing an apron and they told me to fill my apron with coins. You couldn't imagine the money.

I was seventeen when Stan and Julie asked me to babysit their daughter Imogene. I was a nanny to her during the day, and sometimes in the evening, they asked me stay with her while they went out. One night, when Imogene was about three years old, I was babysitting and Julie told me to stay in the bedroom. I was curious. Carefully, I opened the door a crack and peeked out. In all my life I will never forget that money I saw piled on the dining room table. There were piles and piles of bills; I don't even know what kind of bills. Fifties, one hundreds, I don't know. There was a lot of chattering and they didn't notice me. Then about six couples came. I thought it was husbands and wives, but no, it was men with their girlfriends. Every one of the women was blond. They took their money off the table and out the door they went.

After everyone left, I gathered enough courage to open a cedar chest the size of a casket in the dining room. Stanley always asked his men to throw the extra change from the slot machines into it for Imogen. I never saw so much change. It was three-quarters full with half dollars, quarters, dimes, and nickels; no pennies. I could have taken a couple of handfuls and they wouldn't have known, but they were gangsters and I didn't want anything to do with them.

*140 ~ Huntspur and Along the Tracks*

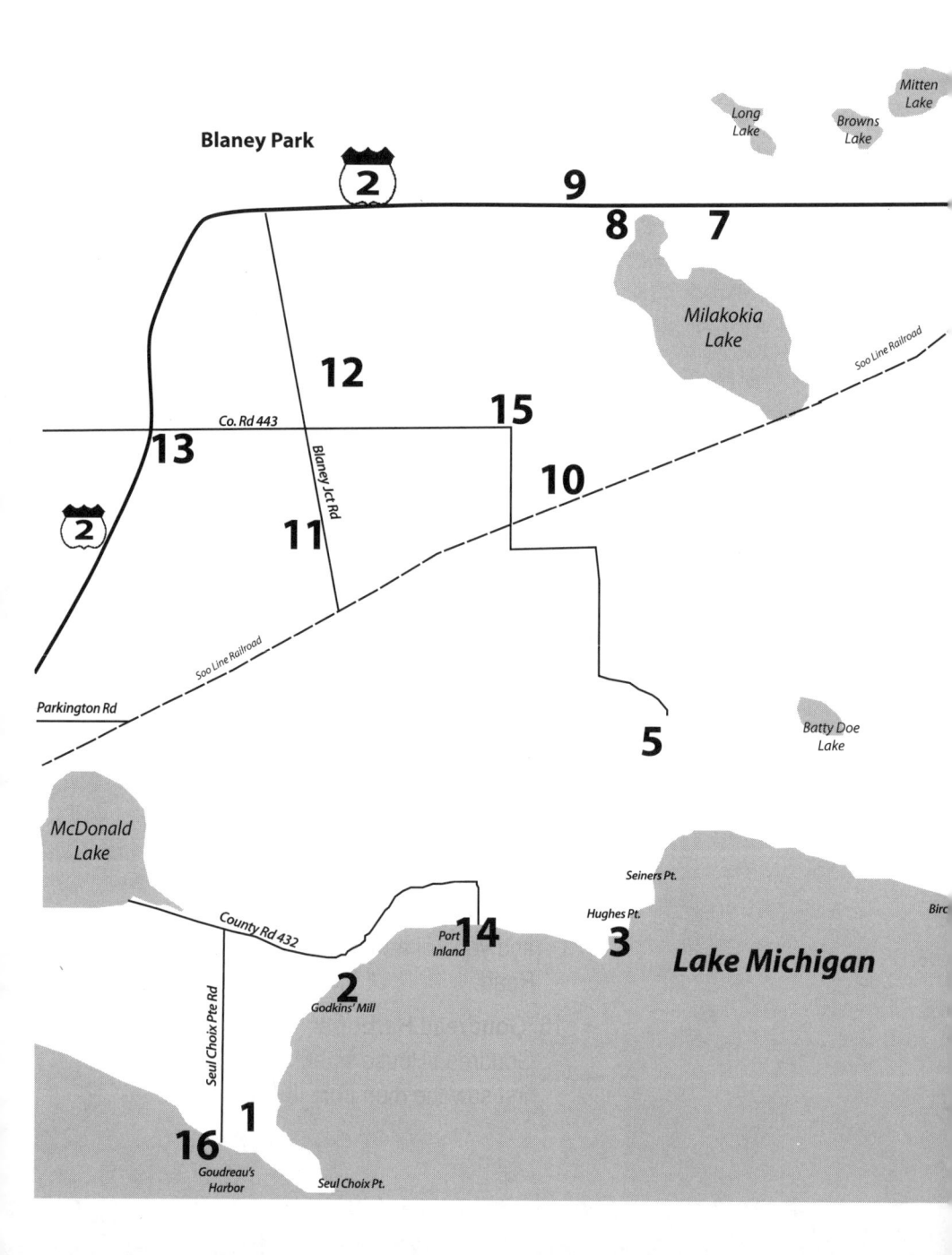

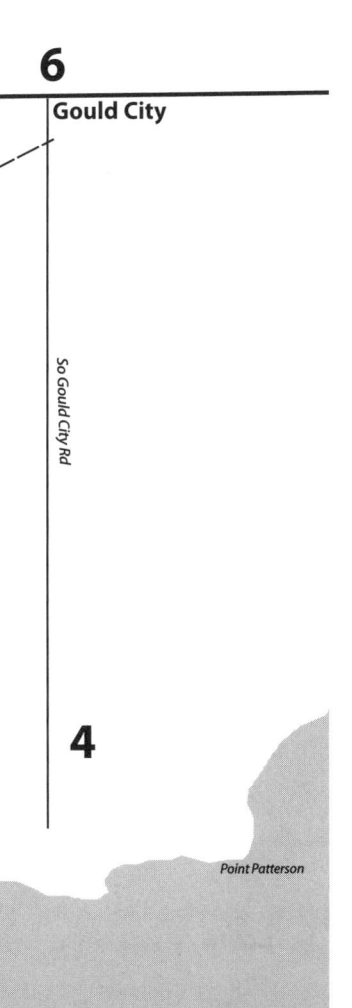

1. **Vern Goudreau house** where Harold Bowman drilled for oil
2. **Godkin's Mill** where Mr. Godkin was fatally cut with a saw
3. **Vanatta's Bay** on the shore of Hughs Point
4. **Newton Township Cemetery** where "hell popped out." Near the northwest corner of the intersection of Leveille Road and South Gould City Road. Eight miles south of US 2 at Gould City.
5. **Porcupine Crossing** Bill Morden got paid more money if he delivered groceries beyond this point.
6. **Gould City** (1/2 mile south of US 2)
7. **Bryan** is overgrown with trees and shrubs and difficult to find
8. **Lee house**
9. **First Lee house**
10. **Huntspur**
11. **Gridley**
12. **Calspar Quarry**
13. **Green School**
14. **Port Inland**
15. **Gate to Quarry** and beginning of Batty Doe Lake Road. Continue along this road and you will arrive at South Gould City Road.
16. **Goudreau Harbor** and site of original Goudreau House where Vern Goudreau first saw the men from the House of David.

## CONCLUSION

Huntspur, like many old logging towns, is gone. House foundations and railroad grades are slowly overgrown with brush and trees, unrecognizable from the forests or fields that surround them. Almost all that is left are photos and some voice recordings of our deceased ancestors, which I wanted to preserve in a book. I believe it's important to document the land's history because it provides information to this generation and future generations about who we are, where we came from, and how we ended up in this remote area of the Upper Peninsula.

My family and many local residents are descendants of the early settlers I interviewed. It was a privilege to record the history that connects generations of families and friends and the places I know so well. That box of old tapes gave me the opportunity to hear the voices of the people who were an important part of my life and the honor to share their stories.

## ABOUT THE AUTHOR

Jane Kopecky was born and raised in Gulliver, Michigan. She is fascinated with local history and enjoys listening to colorful people who can tell a great story. She had several articles published in magazines and was interviewed by NPR about her World War II Conscientious Objectors research.

Jane has a Master's Degree in education from Northern Michigan University and taught for many years in the Manistique Area School district before retiring. She was also a co-owner (along with her husband, John) of Kopecky Well Drilling, now owned by their son.

You may contact Jane at janekopecky@yahoo.com.